KNITTING

KNITTING

BY THE EDITORS OF
LADIES' HOME JOURNAL NEEDLE&CRAFT

MASON / CHARTER   NEW YORK 1977

1 2 3 4 5 6 7 8 9 10

Library of Congress Cataloging in Publication Data

Main entry under title:
Knitting.

   1. Knitting—Patterns. I. Ladies' home
journal needle & craft.
TT820.K6948   746.4'32   77-8172
ISBN 0-88405-474-8
ISBN 0-88405-475-6 pbk.

CONTENTS

7 Introduction

9 Basic Knitting

14 Cover Caps and Scarves

15 FOR MEN AND WOMEN

18 Ribbed Bikini

19 Rainbow Midriff Top

22 Heart-Rimmed Bikini and Skirt

23 Man's Tab-Buttoned Sweater

23 Woman's Tab-Buttoned Tabard

26 Man's Bright-Striped Sweater

27 Man's Bow-Tied V Neck Slipover

30 Man's Checkerboard and Stripe V Neck
   Slipover

31 Sequined Jacket and Cap

34 V Neck Halter and Hat

35 Garter Yoke Pullover and Sleeveless
   Vest

38 Ribbed Cardigan and Tank Top

39 High Pocket Ribbed Pullover

42 Multi-Color Striped Pullover

43 Heart Pullover

46 Fringed Mohair Dress or Skirt

47 Medallion Pullover

50 Rainbow-Striped Pullover and Matching
   Hat

51 Garter-Stitch Cape

54 Mimic Top

55 Braid-Trimmed Vest and Head Scarf

58 Hooded Coat and Matching Skirt

59 Plaid Dress

62 Man's Western-Style Jacket

62 Boy's Striped Sweater

63 Child's Fair Isle Sweater

64 Woman's Fair Isle Sweater

66 Man's Chevron-Striped Sweater

67 Sampler Skirt

70 Reversible Double Knit Ruana

71 Tri-Color Sweater

74 Peruvian Hat

75 Plains Indian Tunic

78 Nomad's Vest

79 Icelandic Shawl-Collar Pullover

82 Icelandic Crew Neck Pullover

83 Tartan Plaid Skirt

86 Red Turtleneck Halter Top

87 Sleeveless V Neck Pullover

91 Chevron-Stitch Skirt and Matching Top

95 Indian Afghan

98 Indian Wraparound

99 FOR THE HOME

102 Diamond Afghan

102 Ripple Runner

103 Quarry-Tile Rug

106 Window Pane Afghan

107 FOR CHILDREN

110 Girl's Sunday-Best Dress and Matching
    Bloomers

110 Teddy's Striped Scarf

111 Child's and Doll's Striped Sweaters

114 Child's Fair Isle Cardigan

114 Child's Fair Isle Pullover

115 Boy's and Teddy Bear's Tennis Sweaters

118 Spot Sweater and Cap

119 Child's Mexican Sweater

122 Cable-Stitched Sweater, Leggings and
    Cap

123 Child and Adult Hat, Mittens and Socks
    Spiral Knit Set

126 Toddler Sweater, Hat, Mittens and
    Socks Spiral Knit Set

127 Bashful Lion

INTRODUCTION

The best part of knitting has to be the knitting itself: feeling the softness of the yarn as it slips through your fingers, being lulled by the rhythm of your hands, tranquilized by the quiet clicking of the needles. It's a soothing way to unwind, something we've remembered to bring with us from a gentler age. And it's satisfying to watch the yarn steadily become what it is to be.

What a peaceful way it is to give yourself a gift that proclaims your love of color and softness and shape and lets you create exactly what you would like to have. (Aren't sweaters what femininity is all about—and afghans the most generous expression of warmth?)

If you're a beginner, you can learn to knit in a night. All you have to have is a ball of yarn and two needles. And all you have to learn is how to cast on, knit, purl, increase, decrease and cast off. You can begin with the scarf on page 110 (even the longest scarf starts with a single stitch). When you develop your skill and courage (the only thing you need to start with is enthusiasm), you can immerse yourself in the intricacies of patterns passed down through time by tradition.

You'll find that to transform nature's tender yarn into an exuberant expression of self is to give pleasure to both hands and heart.

—Joyce Denebrink
Editor, Mason/Charter

BASIC KNITTING

ABBREVIATIONS

The directions are written in abbreviated form, which makes them look both foreign and formidable. Think of the abbreviations as a kind of shorthand and refer to this chart until they become second nature to you.

beg ....begin(ning)

CC ....contrasting color

dble ....double

dec ....decrease

dk ....dark

doz ....dozen·

dp ....double-pointed

gr(s) ....gram(s)

inc ....increase

k ....knit

lp(s) ....loop(s)

lt ....light

MC ....main color

p ....purl

pat ....pattern

psso ....pass slip stitch over

rem ....remain(ing)

rep ....repeat

rnd(s) ....round(s)

sl ....slip

sk ....skip

skn(s) ....skein(s)

st(s) ....stitch(es)

stock ....stockinette

st st ....stockinette stitch

tog ....together

yo ....yarn over

HOW TO CAST ON

This means putting the first row of stitches on the knitting needle. Cast on loosely.

1. Make a slip knot on needle about 12″ from end of yarn. This counts as the first stitch.

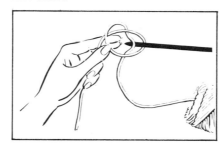

2. Hold needle in right hand.

3. Loop left-hand yarn around thumb.

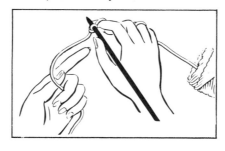

4. Insert needle into loop on thumb.

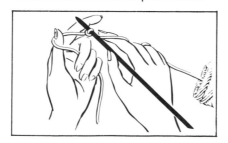

5. Loop right-hand yarn around point of needle.

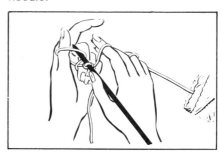

6. Draw yarn through loop on thumb.

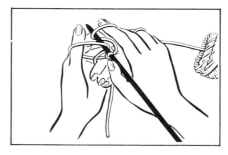

7. Pull yarn in left hand to tighten stitch, easing loop off thumb. Cast on the number of stitches required.

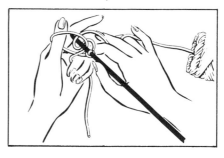

HOW TO KNIT AND PURL

The movements in knitting are the same as in casting on. Push stitches on left needle up toward the point as you work. At end of row the needles change hands: full needle to the left hand, empty needle to the right.

KNIT STITCH
abbr.-k

1. Hold needle with cast-on stitches in left hand, empty needle and yarn in right hand.

2. Slip point of needle into front of first stitch.

3. Loop yarn around point of needle with index finger as you did for casting on.

4. Draw loop through stitch.

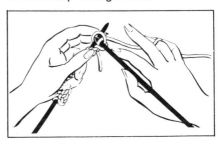

5. Right needle holds new stitch, old stitch is slipped off needle—work all knit stitches in same way.

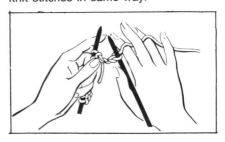

PURL STITCH
abbr.-p

1. Hold needles same as for knit stitch but with yarn in front—slip point of needle in from back of stitch.

2. Loop yarn around point of needle.

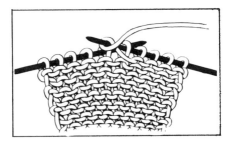

3. Draw yarn through stitch; slip old stitch off left needle—work all purl stitches in same way.

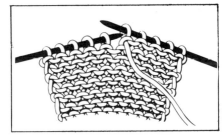

GARTER STITCH

Knit every row.

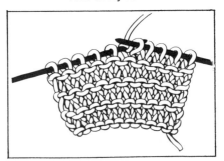

both sides look alike

RIBBING STITCH

RIBBING draws the knitting together, making it elastic . . . It is often used for waist and neckbands. There are two basic types: knit one stitch (k1), bring yarn to front, purl one stitch (p1), take yarn back; repeat to end of row

k1, p1

both sides look alike

. . . or, knit two (k2) and purl two (p2). k2, p2

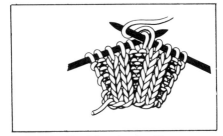

both sides look alike

if row ends with purl start next row with knit.

HOW TO INCREASE

INCREASING
abbr.-inc

in the middle of a row

1. Knit one stitch as usual but do not slip old stitch off left needle . . .

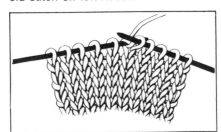

2. . . . now knit a second stitch into the back of the same stitch—slip old stitch off.

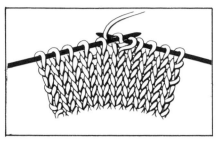

When increasing in the middle, do not make increases on top of each other; this creates bumps in the work. The directions tell you where to increase. If, instead, they say "inc evenly," it means you can choose where to put your increases, as long as they are spaced evenly, and are not directly above the increases on the previous row or round.

INCREASING
at beginning or end of row

Loop yarn around point of needle, as shown.

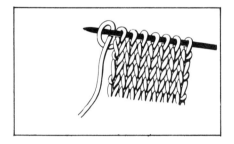

HOW TO DECREASE

There are two ways of decreasing —you must learn both. The knitting instructions tell you which to use.

one way of DECREASING,
abbr.-k2 tog

Knit two stitches together

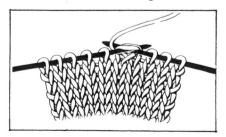

or . . . abbr.-p2 tog

Purl two stitches together

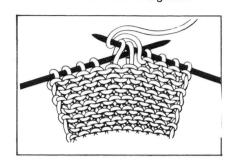

The other way of
DECREASING,
abbr.-sl 1, k 1, p s s o

1. Slip one stitch from left to right needle without knitting, abbr.-sl 1 . . .

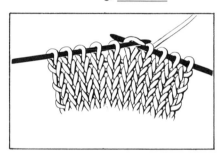

2. . . .knit one stitch, abbr.-k 1 . . .

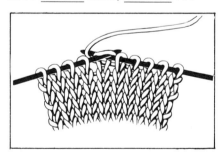

3. . . . with help of left needle, pass the slipped stitch over the knitted stitch, abbr.-p s s o

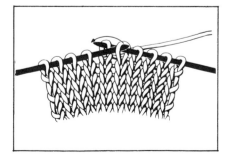

HOW TO BIND OFF
OR CAST OFF

1. Knit two stitches loosely . . . pass first over second stitch and off right needle . . .

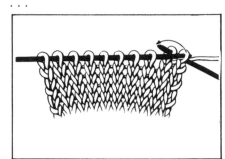

2. . . . one stitch remains on right needle; knit next stitch loosely and repeat . . .

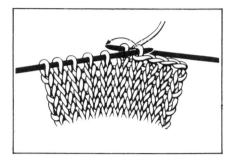

3. bind off all stitches but one; break yarn and draw end through stitch.

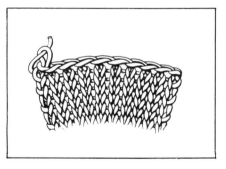

Always bind off in same pattern worked in garment. (To bind off ribbing, knit the knit stitches, purl the purl stitches.) BIND OFF LOOSELY.

HOW TO READ PATTERN DIRECTIONS

Knitting directions tell you everything you need to know about the item you want to make. They tell you what to do—then what you have done. Look them over before you begin; then you'll know what to expect. (After you begin to knit, don't read ahead. It will only confuse you.)

What the symbols mean:

Asterisk (*): Directions immediately following it are to be repeated the given number of times. Example: * k 2 tog; rep from * 3 more times.

Even: Work in same pattern stitch without increasing or decreasing.

Parentheses ( ): Directions within the parentheses should be repeated as often as indicated—(k 2, p 3) 3 times would mean to work what is in ( ) 3 times in all.

Inserting markers: "Sl a marker on a needle," means to put a small safety pin, paper clip or commercial marker on needle. In working, always slip marker from one needle to another. To mark a row or st, tie contrasting yarn at end of row or st.

Slip stitch: Slip stitch from left needle to right without purling or knitting. Insert right-hand needle in st as if to p (unless otherwise specified). Slip stitch from one needle to another being sure that st is not twisted.

HOW TO KEEP TRACK OF WHERE YOU ARE IN THE PATTERN DIRECTIONS

Try one of these methods:

*Place a ruler on the page, just below the row you're working on. Move the ruler down after you complete the row. (If you have children and/or pets, better use a paper-clip instead.)

*Stick straight pins into the page at the beginning and end of each row (this works well with graphs). Move the pins after you complete the row.

*Mark off each row with a pencil as you finish it.

*When you have to make many rows of the same stitch, write the number of each row on a piece of paper, then cross off each number as you complete the row.

*Write out each row on an index card and flip the card over when you finish the row.

*If a pattern is made up of a group of rows to be repeated, put all the rows on one card or put them on separate cards with a rubber band around them.

*If it makes it clearer to you, translate the directions into your own words or rewrite them in your own shorthand. But do it carefully; it's easy to make a mistake.

GAUGE

(6 sts = 1"; 8 rows = 1") Gauge means the number of stitches to the inch and the number of rows to the inch. It is crucial to achieve the right gauge in order for your garment to be the right size. Gauge is determined by the size of the needles and yarn and the tension of the yarn (how easily the yarn slips through your fingers). Using the exact yarn and needle size specified in the directions, work a four inch square. If you have fewer stitches and rows to the inch than required, you knit loosely and should change to a smaller needle; if you have too many stitches and rows to the inch, you knit tightly and should change to a larger needle. Keep changing your needle until your gauge is exactly the same as the gauge specified. **The needle size is not important; the proper gauge is.** That's why directions call for a certain needle size "OR SIZE TO OBTAIN GAUGE."

The size of your stitches may also be affected by your mood. When you are tense, the yarn won't slip through your fingers easily and your stitches will be tight. When you're relaxed, your stitches will be loose. Often people start out knitting tightly, getting looser as they work. To compensate for this, measure the size of your stitches as you work, and switch to a smaller needle if you find your stitches getting looser. In addition, no two people work exactly the same way, so if someone volunteers to help out, you may regret it if you let them.

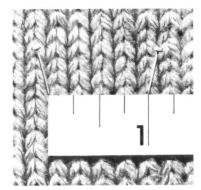

YARN

The directions call for specific brand name yarns and tell you the colors and quantities to use to knit an item exactly like the one you see in the photograph. It is always safest to buy the yarn called for, substitutions may make it difficult for you to obtain the correct gauge. However, if you can obtain the proper gauge—the number of stitches and rows given in the directions—with another yarn, then you can use it.

Buy a yarn that you will enjoy working with, one you

KNITTING NEEDLE SUGGESTED EQUIVALENCY CHART

Canadian Knitting Needles	000	00	0	1	2	3	4	5	6	7	8	9	10	11	12	13	14	15
American Knitting Needles	15	13	12	11	10½	10	9	8	7	6	5	4	3	2	1	0	00	000
Continental Knitting Needles mm (metric)	9	8½	8	7½	7	6½	6	5½	5	4½	4	3½	3/2¾	3/2¾	2½	2¼	2	1¾

like to look at and touch, one that will please you when it is made up. Once you have determined your size—small (medium, large) . . . 3(3,4) skeins—always buy the recommended amount of yarn—or more—so that all the yarn comes from the same dye lot. Save the paper bands or labels. They carry the dye-lot number in case you have to buy more yarn later. Since it is hard to get the same dye lot later, it is better to buy extra yarn at the beginning. Many stores will let you return unused yarn (intact, with a receipt) within a reasonable amount of time. Buy really good yarn if you want; you can always unravel it and re-use it in the future.

The "ply" of a yarn is the number of strands twisted together to make the yarn, and these strands can be of any thickness, so that a 2-ply yarn is not necessarily finer than a 4-ply yarn. Rug yarn is 2-ply or 3-ply and thicker than knitting worsted. Knitting worsted is usually 4-ply. Sport weight yarn is 2-ply or 3-ply or 4-ply, but either way it's about half the thickness of knitting worsted. Fingering yarn and baby yarn are both 3-ply and 4-ply and are thinner than sport weight yarn.

COMPARISON OF OUNCES AND GRAMS

28 grams—approx. 1 oz.
40 grams—approx. 1½ ozs.
50 grams—approx. 1¾ ozs.
100 grams—approx. 3½ ozs.

HOW TO ATTACH NEW YARN

Always join at outer edge of work by making a slip knot with new strand around working strand. Move slip knot up to edge of work and continue knitting. A knot in the center of the work will show and may come undone with wear and tear, and washing.

HOW TO CHANGE COLORS

To prevent holes when working with two or more colors, always pick up color you are about to work from underneath dropped strand.

HOW TO PICK UP STITCHES

This is usually done along an edge of a piece already knitted. Always have right side facing you. Tie yarn to spot where picking up is to start. Work with yarn and one needle only. Insert point of needle through knitting a short distance from the edge, wrap yarn around needle as if to knit and draw loop through piece. Continue across edge, spacing stitches evenly.

HOW TO PICK UP DROPPED STITCHES

Use a crochet hook. In stockinette stitch, insert hook through loop of dropped stitch from front to back of work, hook facing upward. Pull horizontal thread of the row above through loop; repeat to top and place dropped stitch on needle. If pattern stitch is used, pick up stitch in pattern.

HOW TO MEASURE WORK

Spread article on flat surface to required width before measuring the length at center of the piece.

BLOCKING AND STEAMING

This means shaping your finished work. If your project is made of several parts, block the pieces before joining them. Shape each piece to the size you want: you can either draw an outline of the finished shape on heavy paper and shape the piece to that, or you can gently stretch and shape the piece to the measurements specified in the directions. On an ironing board or padded surface, pin each piece in place with plenty of pins placed close together to avoid scalloped edges. **For wool,** steam with a steam iron or through a damp cloth, never letting the iron rest on the piece. **For synthetics, do not iron** (100% acrylic yarns will stretch permanently when steam blocked). Instead, spray the piece thoroughly with water and allow it to dry, pinned out. **Do not block ribbing. Note:** Be sure to use rust-proof pins.

HOW TO WEAVE SEAMS

Hold edges together, right side up. Using matching yarn and large-eyed sewing needle, bring needle up through first st on left edge. Insert needle down through center of first stitch on right edge, pass under 2 rows, draw yarn through to right side. Insert needle in center stitch on corresponding row of left edge, pass under 2 rows as before, draw yarn through to right side. Continue working from side to side, matching rows or patterns. Keep seam flat and elastic.

HOW TO BACK-STITCH SEAMS

Matching rows or patterns, pin right side of pieces together. Take running stitches with a back-stitch about every ½" to keep seams flat

DUPLICATE STITCH

This is used when an additional color or design is desired for a small area. It is worked with tapestry needle over background as shown in diagram rather than knitting it in.

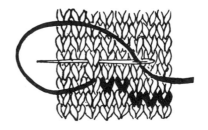

EARFLAP CAP

SIZES: To fit all sizes.

MATERIALS: Bucilla Wool and Shetland Wool (2 oz balls): 1 ball each of Blue (A), Green (B) and Purple (C). Knitting Needles, Nos. 8 and 6 OR SIZE TO OBTAIN GAUGE.

GAUGE: Stockinette St, 5 sts = 1″; 7 rows = 1″.

TO MAKE: With A and No. 6 needles, cast on 87 sts. **Ribbing—Row 1: (wrong side):** P1, * k 1, p 1; rep from * across. **Row 2:** K 1, * p 1, k 1; rep from * across. Rep last 2 rows for 2½″ from beg, end on wrong side. Break off A. Change to No. 8 needles. Join B, decreasing 1 st in first row, work in stockinette st (k 1 row, p 1 row) for 2 rows. **Next Row: (Dec Row):** K 1, * k 10, k 2 tog; rep from * 6 times more, k 1. Work 3 rows even. Having 1 st less before each dec than on previous dec row, make 7 decs evenly spaced on every other row 6 times—37 sts. Work 3 rows even, decreasing 1 st on last row—36 sts. **Next Row:** * K 2 tog; rep from * across. Break yarn, leaving a 15″ end. Using needle, draw end through rem sts and draw up tightly, weave side edges tog—center back seam.

LEFT EARFLAP: With C and No. 8 needles, cast on 27 sts. **Row 1:** (right side): K 5; turn. **Row 2:** Sl 1 st as to p, p 1, k 3. **Row 3:** K 6; turn. **Row 4:** Sl 1 as to p, p 2, k 3. **Row 5:** K 7; turn. **Row 6:** Sl 1 as to p, p across to within last 3 sts, k 3. Continue in this manner knitting 1 more st on each k row until all sts are in work, ending with a k row. Mark end of last row for back edge. **Next Row:** K 3, p to within last 3 sts, k 3. **Next Row:** K across. **Next Row:** K 3, p to within last 3 sts, k 3. Now work dec rows as follows: **Row 1:** K 23, k 2 tog, k 2—26 sts. **Row 2:** K 2, k 2 tog, p across to within last 3 sts, k 3. **Row 3:** K across to within last 4 sts, k 2 tog, k 2. **Row 4:** K 3; turn. **Row 5:** K 3; turn. **Rows 6–13:** Rep last 4 rows (rows 2–5) twice. **Row 14:** K 2, k 2 tog, p across to within last 4 sts, k 2 tog, k 2–18 sts. **Row 15:** K across to within last 4 sts, k 2 tog, k 2–17 sts. **Rows 16–17:** Rep Rows 4–5. **Rows 18–21:** Rep Rows 14–17. **Rows 22–23:** Rep Rows 14–15—10 sts. **Row 24:** K 2, (k 2 tog, k 2) twice. **Row 25:** K 2, (k 2 tog) twice; k 2. Bind off rem 6 sts.

RIGHT EARFLAP: With C and No. 8 needles, cast on 27 sts. **Row 1:** K 3, p 2; turn.

Row 2: Sl 1, k 4. **Row 3:** K 3, p 3; turn. **Row 4:** Sl 1, k 5; turn. **Row 5:** K 3, p 4; turn. Complete to correspond with Left Earflap, reversing shaping.

FINISHING: Sew cast on edge of each earflap under edge of cap at sides, having marked edges meeting at back seam of cap —about 5″ apart at front.

FEATHER STITCH CAP AND SCARF

SIZE: Scarf measures 6″ × 60″. Hat will fit all sizes.

MATERIALS: Bucilla Wool and Shetland Wool (2 oz ball): 3 balls Dk. Green (A), 1 ball each Purple (B), Aqua (C), Med. Green (D). Knitting Needles, No. 8 OR SIZE TO OBTAIN GAUGE.

GAUGE: Stockinette st—5 sts = 1″; 7 rows = 1″.

HAT: With B, cast on 87 sts. K 2 rows. **Pattern: Row 1 (wrong side):** K 1, (k 2 tog) 3 times; * p a st in the horizontal strand between last st used and next st—inc made; p next st, (inc one st as before, p next st) 4 times; inc one st as before (k 2 tog) 6 times; rep from * across, ending last repeat with (k 2 tog) 3 times; k 1. **Row 2:** K across. **Row 3:** K 1, p 85, k 1. **Row 4:** K across. Last 4 rows form pat. **Rows 5–8:** Rep last 4 rows once. Break off B. Attach C. **Rows 9–16:** With C, rep Rows 1 through 4 twice. Break off C. Attach D. **Rows 17–24:** With D, rep Rows 1 through 4 twice. **Rows 25–26:** With D, k 2 rows. Break off D. Attach A. **Row 27:** With A, k across decreasing one st—86 sts. **Row 28:** K 1, p 84, k 1. **Dec Row:** K 1, * k 10, k 2 tog; rep from * across, end with k 1–7 sts decreased. **Next row:** K 1, p across to last st, k 1. **Next Dec Row:** K across, decreasing 7 sts evenly spaced across, having one st less before each dec than previous dec row. Rep last 2 rows alternately until 30 sts rem, end with a p row. **Last row:** * K 2 tog; rep from * across—15 sts. Break off, leaving a 15″ length of yarn. Thread a darning needle with this end and draw through rem sts; pull tightly and fasten, sew ends of rows tog, matching colors.

SCARF: With A, cast on 30 sts. Work in garter st (k each row) until total length is 58″ from beg. Block to 60″ length.

STRIPED CAP AND FRINGED SCARF

SIZE: Scarf measures about 6″ × 74″, including fringe. Hat will fit all sizes.

MATERIALS: Bucilla Wool and Shetland Wool (2 oz ball): 3 balls of Purple Gleam (A). Bucilla Crewel Wool: 2 cards each of #33 Royal (B), #24 Dk Aqua (C), #8 Dk Fern (D), #23 Med. Aqua (E), #98 Sun Yellow (F), #9 Light Rose (G), #15 Dk Pink (H), #92 Scarlet (I), #31 Purple (J). Knitting Needles, 1 pair each Nos. 6 and 8 OR SIZE TO OBTAIN GAUGE.

GAUGE: Ribbing—13 sts = 2″. **Garter st—** 5 sts = 1″; 7 rows = 1″

HAT: BAND: With No. 6 needles and A, cast on 16 sts. **Row 1:** * K 1, p 1; rep from * across. Rep row 1 until piece measures 19½″ from beg. Bind off in ribbing. Along side edge of band with No. 8 needles and B pick up and k 86 sts. K 2 rows with B, continuing in garter st (k each row) work 2 rows each of C, D, E, F. **Next row: Dec row:** Join G, k 1, * k 10, k 2 tog; rep from * 6 times more; k 1. **Next Row:** K across. Break G. Join H, k 2 rows even. Break H. **Next Row: Dec Row:** Join I, k 1, * k 9; k 2 tog; rep from * 6 times more; к 1–7 sts decreased. **Next Row:** K across. Break I. **Next Row: Dec Row:** Join J, k 1, * k 8, k 2 tog; rep from * 6 times more; k 1. **Next Row:** K across. Starting with color B again, continue to work 2 rows of each color in the same sequence, dec 7 sts evenly spaced on first row of color changes, keeping 1 st at each edge and having 1 less st before each dec on each successive dec row until 16 sts rem. Work 2nd row even with next color. **Next Row:** Join next color, * k 2 tog; rep from * across—8 sts. Break yarn, leaving 15″ end. With a darning needle, draw end through rem sts and draw up tightly. Sew side edges tog.

SCARF: With No. 6 needles and A, cast on 39 sts. **Row 1:** P 1, * k 1, p 1; rep from * to end. **Row 2:** K 1, * p 1, k 1; rep from * to end. Rep last 2 rows until 45″ from beg. Bind off in ribbing. Block to about 50″ long. **Fringe:** Wind yarn around a 12″ piece of cardboard, cut at one end. Knot a 3-strand fringe of each color across each end of scarf in the following order: B, C, D, E, A, F, G, H, I, J. **To knot fringe,** hold 3 strands of same color tog, fold in half to form a loop. With a crochet hook draw loop thru a st; draw loose ends through loop and pull tight. Trim fringe evenly.

FOR
MEN AND WOMEN

Delight in the doing, the giving, the wearing. It will replenish the spontaneity of a generous nature.

Here is the cardigan to bring back the cocktail hour . . . a cape with floppy fringe . . . a Fair Isle sweater with a paper doll pattern . . . a skirt that's a dramatic sampler of the needleworker's art . . . boldly-patterned Peruvian hats to knit as descendants of the Incas do . . . a shirt straight off the back of a Plains Indian . . . a wild and wooly nomad's vest . . . two Icelandic sweaters, natural as the elements, true to island tradition . . . and a dress that catches yarn's changing colors in soft curves . . .

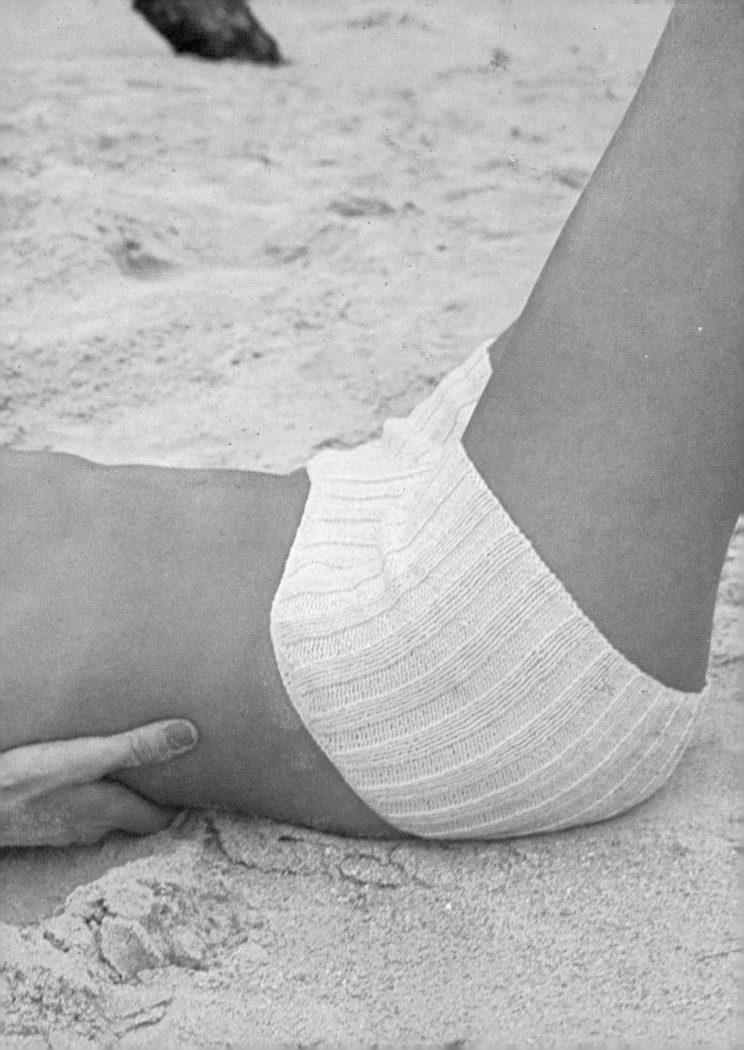

RIBBED BIKINI

SIZE: Directions are for small size (8-10). Changes for medium size (12-14) are in parentheses.

MATERIALS: Reynolds Parfait (30-gr ball), 4 balls all sizes. 1 yd ½" elastic. Elastic sewing thread. Knitting Needles, No. 4 OR SIZE TO OBTAIN GAUGE. Steel Crochet Hook, No. 1.

BLOCKING MEASUREMENTS: Width of pants across front at hips—16 (18)"; across back—17 (19)".

GAUGE: 6 sts = 1"; 10 rows = 1".

PANTS: FRONT: Beg at lower edge, cast on 42 (48) sts for first leg, drop yarn; with another ball of yarn, cast on 42 (48) sts on same needle for second leg. Working on both legs at once, work in k 3, p 3 ribbing, casting on 1 st at inside edge of ea leg (at center of needle) every 3rd row 3 times, working added sts into ribbing—45 (51) sts on ea leg. Work 1 row even. **Joining Row:** Work in ribbing across first leg, with same strand cast on 6 sts for crotch, with same strand continue in ribbing across 2nd leg—96 (108) sts. Cut off extra strand. Continue in ribbing on all sts for 6 (7)" above crotch or desired length. Bind off

loosely in ribbing.

BACK: Working as for front, cast on same number of sts. Work in ribbing of k 3, p 3; cast on 1 st at inside edge of each leg every other row 5 times—47 (53) sts for each leg. **Joining Row:** Work as for front, casting on 8 sts for crotch —102 (114) sts. Complete as for front.

FINISHING: Weave side leg and crotch seams. **Casing For Elastic:** Cut elastic about 1" less than waist size and join into a circle; pin into position around inside of waistline. Holding the knitting over the fingers with elastic slightly stretched, work a herringbone stitch (diagram) over elastic, catching back of sts above and below. If desired run 2 rows of matching elastic thread thru back of sts inside of leg edges.

BRA: Beg at lower edge, cast on 93 (105) sts. **Row 1:** (right side): K 3, * p 3, k 3. Rep from * across. **Row 2:** P 3, * k 3, p 3. Rep from * across. Rep'ing these 2 rows for ribbing, bind off in ribbing 2 sts at beg of next 8 rows. **Next Row:** Bind off 2 sts, work across until 36 (42) sts from bound-off sts, drop yarn; join a second ball of yarn and bind off 1 st. finish row. **Next Row:** Working both

sides at once, bind off 2 sts at beg of row, finish row. Continue in ribbing, dec 1 st ea side of ea piece every 4th row 12 times, every other row 5 (8) times. Bind off rem 2 sts of ea piece.

Back Straps: With dble strand and crochet hook, make lp on hook, work 2 sc on side edge of bra for 15" or desired length. End off. Work other back strap the same.

Shoulder Straps: Make straps in same way at each tip of bra with 2 sc each, long enough to tie around neck. From right side, work 1 row sc over elastic thread at lower edge of bra, dec'ing edge to desired fit. Adjust elastic to fit; tack at ea end.

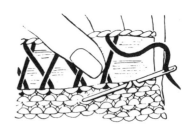

RAINBOW MIDRIFF TOP

SIZES: Directions are for size 10. Changes for size 12 and 14 are in parentheses.

MATERIALS: Brunswick Germantown Knitting Worsted: 1 skn each Strato Blue 4101 (A), Burnt Orange 4061 (B), Orange 406 (C), Persimmon 4060 (D), Saffron 4051 (E), Medium Yellow 4031 (F), Light Yellow 403 (G). Knitting Needles, 1 Pair No. 7 OR SIZE TO OBTAIN GAUGE. Steel Crochet Hook No. 1.

GAUGE: 14 sts = 3"; 7 rows = 1".

BLOCKING MEASUREMENTS: Bust— 33 (35-37)". Width of back or front at underarms—16½ (17½-18½)".

STRIPED PATTERN: Work in stockinette st (k 1 row, p 1 row) 16 (18-20) rows of each color in following sequence: A, B, C, D, E, F, G.

BACK: With No. 7 needles and A cast on 61 (66-71) sts. Work striped pat, inc 1 st each end every 1" 7 times, changing colors as required—75 (80-85) sts. Work even in pat until A, B, C and 8 (10-10) rows of D stripes are completed. Piece should measure approx. 8 (9-10)" from beg. Mark last row.

ARMHOLES: Continuing with D stripe, bind off 5 sts at the beg of next 2 rows. Keeping to striped pat, dec 1 st each end every other row 6 times—53 (58-63) sts. Work even in pat until stripes D, E, F and 8 (10-10) rows of G have been completed. Armholes should measure approximately 7 (7¾-8½)" above marked row

SHOULDERS: With G, bind off 7 (8-8) sts at beg of next 2 rows, then 7 (7-8) sts at beg of next 2 rows. With B, bind off remaining 25 (28-31) sts for back neck.

FRONT: Work same as back until arm-holes measure 2" above marked row (decs completed), ending on wrong side.

NECK AND SHOULDER: Next Row: K first 24 (26-28) sts; bind off center 5 (6-7) sts; join another ball of yarn and k last 24 (26-28) sts. Working both sides at once, dec 1 st at each neck edge on next row, then every 4th row 9 (10-11) times more; **at same time,** when arm-hole measures same as back, bind off 7 (8-8) sts at each armhole edge once, then 7 (7-8) sts once.

FINISHING: Block pieces to measurements. Sew shoulder and side seams matching stripes. From right side, work 1 row sc around lower edge, neck and armholes in corresponding colors, join rnd with sl st in first sc. **Do not turn.** Work 1 row reverse sc from left to right (in opposite direction than last sc row). Join in first sc. End off.

SIZES: Directions are for size 8-10. Changes for size 12-14 are in parentheses.

MATERIALS: Bucilla Twin Pak Knitting Worsted (4 oz Paks): 2 Paks Purple (A); 1 each of Pink (B), Red (C), Light Red (D), Tangerine (E), Turquoise (F) and Lime (G). Knitting needles, 1 pair each Nos. 6 and 8 OR SIZE TO OBTAIN GAUGE. Crochet hook, size H. Round elastic for bikini; ¾" wide elastic, 5 bobbins and hook and eye for skirt.

GAUGE: No. 6 needles—5 sts = 1"; 7 rows = 1". No. 8 needles—9 sts = 2"; 13 rows = 2".

BLOCKING MEASUREMENTS: Bikini: Bust—33 (36)". Upper edge of pants—29 (31)". **Skirt:** Waistline—24 (27)". Width at hips—35 (37)". Width at lower edge—36½ (38½)".

BIKINI: Bra Cup (Make 2): With No. 6 needles and A, cast on 36 (40) sts. Work in stockinette st (p 1 row, k 1 row) for 7 rows, end with p row. Break A. Attach B, work even in stockinette st for 4 rows. Break B. Attach C, and work 4 rows even. Break C. Attach D, work 3 rows even, thus ending with k row. **1st Dec Row:** P 16 (18), (p 2 tog) twice; p 16 (18)—34 (38) sts. **2nd Dec Row:** K 15 (17), (k 2 tog) twice; k to end—2 sts decreased at center of row. Break D. Continuing to dec 2 sts at center of each row, work in stockinette st in following color sequence: 4 rows E, 2 rows F, 9 (11) rows G. Bind off rem 2 sts. **Joining Cups and Ties:** With right side facing, using crochet hook and F, work sc evenly along lower edge of right cup, ch 1, sc evenly along lower edge of left cup; make a chain 17" long for tie; sl st in 2nd ch from hook and in each ch, sc in same place as last sc made on left cup. * Sc along side edge of cup to point; make a chain 17" long for tie; sl st in 2nd ch from hook and each ch across, sc in point of cup and continue to sc along other side edge of same cup, sc in ch-1 between cups; working along edges of right cup, rep from * once but end with sc in same place as first sc made on right cup; make another tie at lower edge as before. Join with sl st to first sc. Break off and fasten.

PANTS: Crotch and Front: Start at crotch edge with No. 6 needles and F, cast on 17 sts. Work in stockinette st (p 1 row, k 1 row) for 21 (23) rows, thus ending with p row. **Next Row (right side):** Inc one st in first st, k to within 2 sts of end, inc one st in next st, k 1. **Next Row:** P across, increasing one st each side. Break F. Continue in stockinette st throughout. Increasing one st each side every row 9 (13) times more; then every other row 12 (11) times work in the following color sequence: 7 (9) rows G, 7 rows A, 4 rows B, 4 rows C, 5 rows D, 4 rows E, 2 rows F—63 (69) sts. Break F. Attach A and p 1 row. Cut 4 one-yd strands for hearts. **NOTE:** Use

a separate strand for each heart; carry A loosely along wrong side. When changing colors, twist unused color around the other once to prevent making holes.

Heart Pat: Row 1: With A, k 16 (19), * attach C and k 1; with A, k 9; rep from * twice more; attach C and k 1; with A, k 16 (19). Starting with 2nd row, follow Chart 1 for each heart to end of row 6. Break C strands. With A, work 2 rows even. Bind off loosely.

BACK: With right side facing, using C, pick up and k 17 sts along the cast-on edge of crotch. Working in the following color sequence: 4 rows C, 5 rows D, 4 rows E, 2 rows F, 7 (9) rows G, 7 rows A, 4 rows B, 4 rows C, 5 rows D, 4 rows E, 2 rows F; inc one st each side every row 18 (22) times; then every other row 11 (10) times; every 4th row twice—79 (85) sts. Break F. Attach A and p 1 row.

Heart Pat: Cut 5 one-yd strands of C. **Row 1:** With A, k 19 (22), *attach C and k 1; with A, k 9; rep from * 3 times more; attach C and k 1; with A, k 19 (22). Follow Chart 1 same as for Front. With A, work 2 rows even. Bind off loosely.

FINISHING: Steam pieces lightly through a damp cloth. **Edging:** With right side facing, using crochet hook and F, work 1 row of sc along each side edge of front, crotch and back, easing in edge slightly. Sew side seams from beg of heart stripe to top edge. Wtih right side facing, attach F to top end of a side seam, hold 2 strands of round elastic along top edge, working over elastic, sc evenly along top edge of pants to within 1" from end. Adjust elastic to fit; allowing 1 inch for sewing, cut elastic; overlap ends and sew for 1". Complete sc row. Join with sl st to first sc. Break off and fasten.

SKIRT: Wind 5 bobbins with C for hearts (see note on Pants directions). Start at lower edge with No. 8 needles and A, cast on 161 (171) sts. Work in stockinette st (p 1 row, k 1 row) for 15 rows, thus ending with p row.

Heart Pat: Row 1: With A, k 18(23), * attach C and k 1; with A, k 30; rep from * 3 times more; attach C and k 1; with A, k 18(23). Starting with row 2 and working in stockinette st throughout, follow Chart 2 for each heart through row 19. Break C strands. With A, work 17 rows even, decreasing 8(10) sts evenly spaced on last row, end with p row—153(161) sts. Work even in following color sequence: *6 rows B, 6 rows C, 8 rows D, 6 rows E, 4 rows F, 10 rows G, 12 rows A; rep color sequence from * until length is 27" from beg or 8" less than desired finished length, end with p row.

Side Dart: Continuing in the same color sequence throughout work as follows: **Dec Row:** K 34(36), k 2 tog, place a marker on needle, k 1, sl 1, k 1, p s s o, k 75(79); k 2 tog, place a marker on needle, k 1, sl 1, k 1, p s s o, k 34(36)—2 sts decreased at each side. Carry markers. Work 5 rows even. **Next Dec Row:** * K to within 2 sts before next marker, k 2 tog, slip marker, k 1, sl 1, k 1, p s s o; rep from * once, k to end. Continue in color sequence; rep last Dec Row every 6th row 3 times more; then every 4th row 6(5) times. Work 2(6) rows even, end with k row. **Next Row:** K in back of each st across for turning ridge. Change to No. 6 needles. Starting with a k row, work even in stockinette st for 6 rows for facing. Bind off loosely.

FINISHING: Steam lightly through a damp cloth to measurements. Turn waist facing to wrong side at turning ridge and sew in place. Cut the ¾" elastic to desired waist measurement. Insert elastic and secure at each end of facing. **Edging:** With right side facing, using crochet hook and F, sc evenly along front and lower edges. Break off and fasten. **Ties:** Attach F to end of waist edge, ¾" below top edge; make a chain 24" long; sl st in 2nd ch from hook and in each ch to within last 5 ch sts, ch 5 and join with sl st to top corner of front edge. Break off and fasten. Make tie at opposite edge in same way. Sew hook and eye at waist edge.

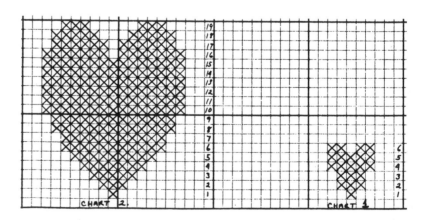

MAN'S TAB-BUTTONED SWEATER

SIZES: Directions are for Size 38. Changes for Sizes 40, 42 and 44 are in parentheses.

MATERIALS: Unger's Harmonie, 1.35 oz. ball—10 (11, 12, 13) balls. Knitting needles Nos. 3 and 5, OR SIZE TO OBTAIN GIVEN GAUGE. Size E aluminum crochet hook. 2 Buttons, ¾".

GAUGE: 11 sts = 2".

BACK: With No. 3 needles, cast on 106 (114, 118, 122) sts. Work in k 2, p 2 ribbing for 2", increasing 1 st each end of last row for size 38 and 44—108 (114, 118, 124) sts. Change to No. 5 needles and Garter St (k every row). Work even until 17" from beg. or desired length to underarm.

SHAPE ARMHOLES: Bind off 6 (7, 7, 7) sts beg next 2 rows. Dec 1 st each end every other row 6 (6, 6, 7) times—84 (88, 92, 96) sts. Work even until armholes measure 8 (8½, 9, 9½)".

SHAPE NECK: K 25 (26, 27, 28) sts, attach another ball of yarn, bind off center 34 (36, 38, 40) sts, k 25 (26, 27, 28) sts. Work both sides at the same time until armholes measure 8¾ (9¼, 9¾, 10¼)". Bind off the 25 (26, 27, 28) sts on each side.

FRONT: Work same as back to underarm.

SHAPE ARMHOLES AND SIDE OPENING: Bind off 6 (7, 7, 7) sts, k until there are 76 (79, 82, 86) sts on needle for left side. Slip remaining 26 (28, 29, 31) sts to a holder for right side. Dec 1 st at armhole edge every other row 6 (6, 6, 7) times—70 (73, 76, 79) sts. Work until armhole measures 5(5½, 6, 6½)", ending at front opening. **Buttonhole Row 1:** K 4, bind off next 3 sts, k to end. **Row 2:** K, casting on 3 sts above bound off sts of previous row. Work until armhole measures 5½ (6, 6½, 7)", ending at front opening. **SHAPE NECK:** K 11 sts and slip onto a holder for flap, bind off center 34 (36, 38, 40) sts, k remaining 25 (26, 27, 28) sts. Work even until armhole is same as back to shoulder. Bind off. Slip the 26 (28, 29, 31) sts from holder onto needle for right side. Cast on 11 sts at front opening, k 26 (28, 29, 31) sts—37 (39, 40, 42) sts. Shape armhole at arm edge as for left side—25(26, 27, 28) sts. Work until armhole measures same as for back to shoulder. Bind off.

FLAP: Slip the 11 sts from holder onto needle. Work Garter St for 3". **Buttonhole and Top Shaping: Row 1:** K 2 tog, k 2, bind off next 3 sts, k 2, k 2 tog. **Row 2:** K across, casting on 3 sts above bound off sts of previous row. **Row 3:** K 2 tog, k 5, k 2 tog. **Row 4:** K. **Row 5:** K 2 tog, k 3, k 2 tog. **Row 6:** K. **Row 7:** K 2 tog, k 1, k 2 tog. Bind off.

SLEEVES: With No. 3 needles, cast on 54 (58, 62, 66) sts. Work in k 2, p 2 ribbing for 3". Change to No. 5 needles and Garter St, increasing 5 sts evenly across first row—59 (63, 67, 71) sts. Work even 1½". Inc 1 st each end of next row, then every 1½" for 8 times more—77(81, 85, 89) sts. Work even until 20" from beg, or 1" more than desired length to underarm

SHAPE CAP: Bind off 6 (7, 7, 7) sts beg next 2 rows. Dec 1 st each end every other row 24 (25, 26, 27) times. Bind off 2 sts beg next 4 rows. Bind off.

FINISHING: Sew shoulder, side and sleeve seams. Overlap left side of front over right side at base of opening and sew. Sew on buttons. With right side facing, work 1 row of sc around opening, neck and flap. DO NOT BLOCK OR PRESS. Wet block (wet with cold water. Lay on a towel to measurements. Dry away from heat and sun).

WOMAN'S TAB-BUTTONED TABARD

SIZES: Directions are for Size 8. Changes for Sizes 10, 12 and 14 are in parentheses.

MATERIALS: Unger's Harmonie, 1.35 oz. ball—10 (11, 12, 13) balls. Knitting needles No. 4, OR SIZE TO OBTAIN GIVEN GAUGE. Size E aluminum crochet hook. 3 Buttons, ¾".

GAUGE: 13 sts = 2".

BACK: Cast on 121 (127, 133, 139) sts. Work Garter St (k every row) for 11 rows. **Row 1:** K. **Row 2:** K 8, p to within last 8 sts, k 8. Repeat Rows 1 and 2 for pattern. Work even until 3" from beg, ending with Row 2. **Dec Row:** K 8, sl 1, k 1, psso, k to last 10 sts, k 2 tog, k 8. Repeat Dec Row every 3" for 7 times more—105 (111, 117, 123) sts. Work even until 29" from beg, or desired length to underarm.

SHAPE ARMHOLES: Bind off 7 (7, 8, 8) sts beg next 2 rows. Dec 1 st each end every other row 6 (7, 7, 8) times—79 (83, 87, 91) sts. Work even until armholes measure 5 (5¼, 5½, 5¾)", ending on right side.

SHAPE NECK: Row 1: Wrong side. P 15 (16, 17, 18) sts, k next 49 (51, 53, 55) sts, p 15 (16, 17, 18) sts. **Row 2:** K. Repeat Rows 1 and 2 for 4 times more (8 rows). **Next row:** K 23 (24, 25, 26) sts, and sl onto a holder, bind off center 33 (35, 37, 39) sts, k 23 (24, 25, 26) sts. **Next row:** P 15 (16, 17, 18), k 8. **Next row:** K. Repeat last 2 rows until entire armhole measures 6¾ (7, 7¼, 7½)".

SHAPE SHOULDER: At arm edge, bind off 7 (8, 8, 8) sts every other row 1 (3, 2, 1) time, 8 (0, 9, 9) sts 2 (0, 1, 2) times. Slip sts from holder to needle, attach yarn at neck edge, work to correspond to other side.

FRONT: Work same as back to within 2" of underarm—105 (111, 117, 123) sts.

FRONT OPENING: K 25 (27, 29, 31) sts, cast on 11 sts—36 (38, 40, 42) sts. Sl remaining 80 (84, 88, 92) sts to a holder. **Next row:** K 8, p to last 8 sts, k 8. **Next row:** K. Repeat last 2 rows until same length as back to underarm.

SHAPE ARMHOLE: At arm edge, bind off 7 (7, 8, 8) sts, then dec 1 st every other row 6 (7, 7, 8) times—23 (24, 25, 26) sts. Work until armhole measures same as back to shoulder. At arm edge, bind off 7 (8, 8, 8) sts every other row 1 (3, 2, 1) time, 8 (0, 9, 9) sts 2 (0, 1, 2) times. Slip the 80 (84, 88, 92) sts from holder onto needle. Attach yarn at opening edge. **Row 1:** K. **Row 2:** K 8, p to last 8 sts, k 8 (front opening). Keeping the 8 sts at front edge in Garter St and 8 sts at seam edge in Garter St, work to underarm as back.

SHAPE ARMHOLE: At arm edge, bind off 7 (7, 8, 8) sts once, then dec 1 st every other row 6 (7, 7, 8) times—67 (70, 73, 76) sts. Work even until armhole measures 3 (3¼, 3½, 3¾)", ending on right side. **Next row:** P 15 (16, 17, 18) sts, k remaining 52 (54, 56, 58) sts. Work 4 rows more, keeping neck sts in Garter St as established. **Buttonhole Row 1:** K 4, bind off next 3 sts, complete row. **Row 2:** Work as established, casting on 3 sts above bound off sts of previous row. Work 4 rows more as established.

SHAPE NECK: K 11 sts and sl to a holder at neck edge for flap, bind off center 33 (35, 37, 39) sts, k remaining 23 (24, 25, 26) sts. Work on these sts only, keeping 8 sts at neck edge in Garter St until armhole is same as back to shoulder.

SHAPE SHOULDER: At arm edge, bind off 7 (8, 8, 8) sts every other row 1 (3, 2, 1) time, 8 (0, 9, 9) sts 2 (0, 1, 2) times.

FLAP: Sl 11 sts from holder onto needle. Work Garter St for 2½". **Buttonhole and Top Shaping: Row 1:** K 2 tog, k 2, bind off next 3 sts, k 2, k 2 tog. **Row 2:** K, casting on 3 sts over bound off sts of previous row. **Row 3:** K 2 tog, k 5, k 2 tog. **Row 4:** K. **Row 5:** K 2 tog, k 3, k 2 tog. **Row 6:** K. **Row 7:** K 2 tog, k 1, k 2 tog. Bind off.

SLEEVES: Cast on 87 (91, 95, 99) sts. Work Garter St for 11 rows. Change to Stock St. Work 4 rows even. Dec 1 st each end of next row, then every 4th row 6 times more—73 (77, 81, 85) sts. Work 3 more rows.

SHAPE CAP: Bind off 7 (7, 8, 8) sts beg next 2 rows. Dec 1 st each end every other row 20 (21, 22, 23) times. Bind off 3 sts beg next 4 rows. Bind off.

FINISHING: Sew shoulder and sleeve seams. Sew ½" of side seams from underarm down. Sew in sleeves. With right side facing, work 1 row of sc around front opening, flap and neck edge. Buttonhole st around buttonholes. Sew on buttons. Overlap right side of opening over left and sew, then sew a button through both thicknesses 1" above start of opening.

TIES: Make 4, or as many as desired for side closing. Cast on 90 sts. Work Garter St. for ¾". Bind off. Sew a tie to each side for closing. DO NOT BLOCK OR PRESS. Wet block (wet with cold water. Lay on a towel to measurements. Dry away from heat and sun).

MAN'S BRIGHT-STRIPED SWEATER

SIZES: Directions are for size 38. Changes for sizes 40, 42, and 44 are in parentheses.

MATERIALS: Bernat Berella Sportspun (2 oz. ball). 7 (7–8–8) Natural A, 1 each of Green B, Red C, Navy D. No. 4 and No. 6 knitting needles OR SIZE TO OBTAIN GIVEN GAUGE.

GAUGE: 5½ sts = 1", 7 rows = 1".

BACK: With No. 4 needles and B cast on 105 (111–115–121) sts. **Row 1(right side):** K 1, *P 1, K 1, rep from * across. **Row 2:** P 1, *K 1, P 1, rep from * across. Break off B, join C. **Row 3:** With C, knit. **Row 4:** With C rep Row 2. Break off C, join D. **Row 5:** With D knit. **Row 6:** With D rep Row 2. **Row 7:** With D rep Row 1. With D continue in rib pat to 3", ending with Row 2. Break off D, join C. With C rep Rows 3 and 4. Break off C, join B. With B rep Rows 3 and 4. Break off B, join A. Change to No. 6 needles and Stock st. Working with A only, work to 16½" from beg ending ready for a right side row.

SHAPE ARMHOLES: Bind off 5 (6–6–7) sts at beg of next 2 rows. Dec 1 st each end every other row 6 times. 83 (87–91–95) sts.

Work until armholes measure 8½ (9–9½–10)", ending ready for a right side row.

SHAPE SHOULDERS: Bind off 6 (7–7–7) sts at beg of next 2 (8–6–4) rows, 7 (0–8–8) sts at beg of next 6 (0–2–4) rows. Place remaining 29 (31–33–35) sts on a holder for back of neck.

FRONT: Work same as back until there are 12 rows less than back to underarm. Keeping to Stock st work 2 rows C, 8 rows B. Break off C and B. Work 4 rows A. Shape armholes as on back. Work until armholes measure 4½ (5–5½–6)" ending ready for a right side row.

SHAPE NECK: K 32 (33–34–35) sts, sl center 19 (21–23–25) sts on a holder, join a 2nd ball A, K 32 (33–34–35) sts. Working both sides at once, dec 1 st at neck edge every other row 5 times. Work on 27 (28–29–30) sts (each side) until armholes measure as back to shoulder. Shape shoulders as on back.

SLEEVES: With No. 4 needles and C cast on 51 (55–57–61) sts. With C rep Rows 1 and 2 of back. Drop C, join A. * With A rep Rows

3 and 4, then 1 and 2 of back. Drop A, pick up C. With C rep Rows 3 and 4 of back. Rep from * twice more. Break off C. With A Rep Rows 3 and 4, then 1 and 2 of back. Break off A, join B. Change to No. 6 needles and Stock st. Working with B, inc 1 st each end of first row then every 1" 13 times more. 79 (83–85–89) sts. Work 22 rows B, 4 rows A (2 rows C, 4 rows A) 3 times, 18 rows D. Continue in Stock st with A. Work to 19" from beg or desired length to underarm, ending ready for a right side row.

SHAPE CAP: Bind off 5 (6–6–7) sts at beg of next 2 rows. Dec 1 st each end every other row 19 (20–21–22) times. Bind off 2 sts at beg of next 4 rows. Bind off remaining sts.

FINISHING: Sew left shoulder seam.

NECKBAND: From right side with No. 4 needles and A, beg at right back shoulder pick up 94 (98–102–106) sts around entire neck edge including sts on holder. Break off A, join D. With D purl 1 row. Work in K 1, P 1 ribbing to 2½". Bind off loosely in ribbing. Sew right shoulder, neckband, side and sleeve seams. Sew in sleeves. Fold neckband in half to inside and sew down. **Block.**

MAN'S BOW-TIED V NECK SLIPOVER

SIZES: Directions are for Small (36-38). Changes for Medium (40-42) and Large (44-46) are in parentheses.

MATERIALS: Bernat Berella Sportspun, 2 oz. ball—4 (4, 5) White (MC) and 1 Cranberry (CC). Bernat Aero knitting needles Nos. 4 and 6, OR SIZE TO OBTAIN GAUGE.

GAUGE: 11 sts = 2"; 7 rows = 1".

NOTE: Pattern is embroidered with CC in duplicate st (page 13) when pieces are completed.

BACK: With No 4 needles and CC, cast on 98 (108, 118) sts. Work in k 1, p 1 ribbing for 4 rows. Fasten off CC, attach MC. *With MC, k 1 row, then work 4 rows of ribbing as established. With CC, p next row, then work 4 rows in ribbing with CC as established. Repeat from * once more, increasing 1 st at end of last row — 99 (109, 119) sts. Change to No. 6 needle and MC. Mark center st. Work even in stock. st until 15½" from beg, or desired length to underarm. **SHAPE ARMHOLES:** Bind off 4 (5, 6) sts beg next 4 rows. Dec 1 st each end every other row 4 times — 75 (81, 87) sts. Work even until armholes measure 9 (9½, 10)". **SHAPE SHOULDERS:** Bind off 7 (8, 8) sts beg next 4 rows, then 7 (7, 9) sts beg next 2 rows — 33 (35, 37) sts. Place remaining sts on a holder.

FRONT: Work same as back until completion of armhole shaping, ending with a p row — 75 (81, 87) sts. **SHAPE NECK AND SHOULDERS:** K 37 (40, 43) sts, place center st on a holder, attach another ball MC, k 37 (40, 43) sts. Work both sides at the same time. P 1 row. Next row: Dec 1 st at each neck edge, then every 4th row 10 (11, 12) times more, every other row 5 times — 21 (23, 25) sts. When same length as back to shoulder, at each arm edge, bind off 7 (8, 8) sts every other row twice, 7 (7, 9) sts once.

FINISHING: Starting at center st, duplicate st design on back and front, following chart. Sew left shoulder seam.

NECKBAND: With right side facing, No. 4 needle and MC, k 33 (35, 37) sts from back neck holder, pick up and k 55 (57, 59) sts along left front neck to center, k center st from holder and mark, pick up and k 55 (57, 59) sts along other side of V neck. **Row 1:** P 1, k 1 ribbing to within 2 sts from center st, k 2 tog, p center st, k 2 tog, p 1, k 1 ribbing to end of row. Continue to ribbing to end of row. Continue to work in this manner, decreasing 1 st each side of center st on every row, as follows: 3 more rows MC in ribbing, p 1 row CC, 4 rows CC in ribbing as established. Bind off in ribbing. Sew right shoulder and neckband. **ARMBANDS:** With No. 4 needle, MC and right side facing, pick up and k 114 (118, 122) sts around entire armhole. Fasten off MC, attach CC. P 1 row CC, then work 4 rows of k 1, p 1 ribbing. Bind off in ribbing. Sew side seams in corresponding colors. Steam lightly. **DO NOT BLOCK OR PRESS.**

CHART FOR ALL SIZES

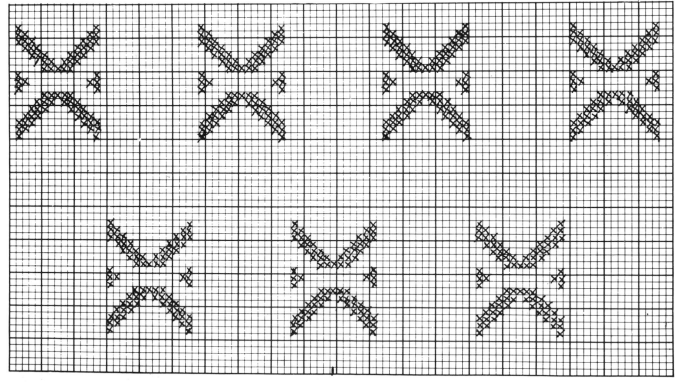

DIAGRAM FOR BOW-TIE DESIGN   CENTER STITCH   X = KEY CC (CRANBERRY)   ☐ = KEY MC (WHITE)

MAN'S CHECKERBOARD AND STRIPE V NECK SLIPOVER

SIZES: Directions are for Small (36-38). Changes for Medium (40-42) and Large (44-46) are in parentheses.

MATERIALS: Bernat Berella Sportspun, 2 oz. ball — 3 (4, 4) White (MC), 2 Black (A) and 1 Scarlet (B). Bernat Aero knitting needles, Nos. 4 and 6, OR SIZE TO OBTAIN GAUGE.

GAUGE: 11 sts = 2"; 7 rows = 1".

NOTE: Carry yarns loosely across back of work to prevent drawing in.

BOX PATTERN: Rows 1 and 3: * K 3 MC, k 3 A; repeat from * across. **Rows 2 and 4:** * P 3 A, p 3 MC; repeat from * across. **Rows 5 and 7:** * K 3 A, k 3 MC; repeat from * across. **Rows 6 and 8:** * P 3 MC, p 3 A; repeat from * across. Repeat these 8 rows for Box Pattern.

STRIPE PATTERN: Work in stock. st in following color sequence: 2 rows MC, 2 rows A.

BACK: With No. 4 needles and MC, cast on 102 (106, 118) sts. **Row 1:** K 2, * p 2, k 2; repeat from * across. **Row 2:** P 2, * k 2, p 2; repeat from * across. Repeat these 2 rows for 4" of ribbing. On last row of medium and large size, inc 1 st each end — 108 — 120 sts. Change to No. 6 needle and Box Pattern. Work 28 rows of Box Pattern. Fasten off MC and A, attach B. Work 4 rows of stock.

st with B. Fasten off B. Change to Stripe Pattern, carrying yarn loosely along side edge when not in use. Work even until 15 (15½, 16)" from beg, or desired length to underarm. **SHAPE ARMHOLES:** Bind off 6 (6, 9) sts beg next 2 rows. Dec 1 st each end every other row 6 (7, 8) times — 78 (82, 86) sts. Work even until entire armhole measures 9 (9½, 10)". **SHAPE SHOULDERS:** Bind off 8 sts beg next 4 rows, then 8 (9, 10) sts beg next 2 rows — 30 (32, 34) sts. **BACK NECKBAND:** Change to No. 4 needle and MC. **For Small and Large:** Work in k 2, p 2 ribbing for 8 rows. Bind off in ribbing. **For Medium: Row 1:** K 1, * p 2, k 2; repeat from *, end k 1. **Row 2:** P 1, * k 2, p 2; repeat from *, end p 1. Repeat these 2 rows until there are 8 rows. Bind off in ribbing.

FRONT: Work same as for back to within 1 p row before underarm. **SHAPE NECK AND ARMHOLE: Next Row:** P 49 (52, 58) sts and place on a holder for right side; p 4 and place on a holder (to be worked into neckband later); p remaining 49 (52, 58) sts for left side. **Next row:** At arm edge, bind off 6 (6, 9) sts, work to within 2 sts from neck edge, k 2 tog (neck dec). Dec 1 st at arm edge every other row 6 (7, 8) times, **at the same time,** dec 1 st at neck edge

every 6th row 4 times more, every 4th row 8 (9, 10) times — 24 (25, 26) sts. Work even to shoulder shaping as for back. **SHAPE SHOULDER:** At arm edge, bind off 8 sts every other row twice, 8 (9, 10) sts once. Place the 49 (52, 58) sts from holder for right side onto needle. Attach yarn at neck edge and work to correspond to other side, reversing shaping.

FRONT NECKBAND: With right side facing, No. 4 needle and MC, pick up and k 62 (66, 70) sts along one side of V, place a marker, k 4 sts from holder for center, place a marker, pick up and k 62 (66, 70) sts along other side of V. **Row 1:** K 2, p 2 ribbing to within 2 sts of first marker, k 2 tog, slip marker, p center 4 sts, slip marker, k 2 tog, p 2, k 2 rib to end of row. Continue in ribbing as established, decreasing 1 st each side of the 4 center stock. sts on every row until you have same number of rows as on back neckband. Bind off in ribbing.

FINISHING: Sew shoulder and neckband seams. **ARMBANDS:** With No. 4 needle, right side facing and MC, pick up and k 114 (118, 126) sts around entire armhole. Work in k 2, p 2 ribbing for 7 rows. Bind off in ribbing. Sew side seams. Steam lightly. **DO NOT BLOCK OR PRESS.**

SEQUINED JACKET AND CAP

SIZES: Directions are for small (8-10) size. Changes for medium (12-14) size are in parentheses. Cap will fit all sizes.

MATERIALS: Bernat Berella 3-Ply Fingering (1 oz. skeins) 60% Orlon—40% Nylon. 13 (15) skns #7094 Black. Knitting needles, 1 pair each Nos. 2 and 3 OR SIZE TO OBTAIN GAUGE. Crochet Hook, Size D. 4 buttons, ⅝" in diameter. 13 (15) strands of 8 mm gold sequins.

GAUGE: 7 sts = 1"; 10 rows = 1".

FINISHED MEASUREMENTS: Bust — 33(37)". Width of back at underarm — 16(18)"; width of each front at underarm (excluding band)—8(9)"; width of sleeve at upper arm—11½(12½)".

NOTE: Slip-knot the sequin string to yarn and slide sequins onto yarn with inside of cup facing ball of yarn. Thread a few hundred at a time and slide them gently over slubs in yarn. When knitting the stitch with the sequin, place sequin close to work and knit into the back of stitch. Jacket is worked in st st (k 1 row, p 1 row). Only the knitted rows are shown on the Chart. The back rows are purled rows throughout (worked without sequins).

JACKET: BACK: Start at inner edge of hem with No. 2 needles, cast on 113 (127) sts. Work in plain st st (k 1 row, p 1 row) for 1" for hem, ending with a k row. K next row for hemline. Change to No. 3 needles and work in pat, following Chart as follows: **Row 1 (right side):** Chart shows half of back; start at right-hand side line on first row indicating size being made and work across to center st; then sk center st and follow same row back in reverse order to starting line. P 2nd and all wrong-side rows (not showing on Chart) without sequins. Work this way until top of Chart is reached; rep first through 16th rows of Chart for pat. Work in pat until length is 16" from hemline, ending with a p row.

ARMHOLES: Being very careful to keep continuity of pat throughout, bind off 6 sts at beg of next 2 rows. Dec one st each end every other row 3(5) times. Work even over rem 95(105) sts until length of armhole is 7(8)", ending with a p row.

SHOULDERS: Keeping in pat, bind off 8(9) sts at beg of next 2 rows. **Next Row:** Bind off 8(9) sts; work in pat until there are 17(19) sts on right-hand needle; place rem 54(59) sts on a stitch holder; turn. Working over sts on needle only, dec one st at neck edge every row 3 times, **at the same time,** from armhole edge, bind off 7 sts every other row twice. Slip sts from holder onto a No. 3 needle; attach yarn, bind off

center 29(31) sts for back of neck and work to correspond with opposite side, reversing shaping.

LEFT FRONT: Start at inner edge of hem with No. 2 needles, cast on 57(64) sts. Work same as for Back until hemline has been made. Change to No. 3 needles. Chart shows entire pat for Front, st marked center st is center front edge of Front. Follow first and all right-side rows from line indicating size being made, across to center front edge. P all wrong-side rows. Work in pat until 14" from hemline, ending at side edge.

NECK: Row 1: Work in pat across to within last 2 sts, **k 2 tog – dec made at front edge.** Keeping continuity of pat, dec one st at front edge every 4th row 5 more times, or until same length as Back to underarm, ending at side edge.

ARMHOLE: Keeping in pat, at side edge, bind off 6 sts at beg of next row. Continuing to dec one st at front edge every 4th row as before, **AT THE SAME TIME,** dec one st at armhole edge every other row 3(5) times. Keeping armhole edge straight, continue to dec one st at front edge every 4th row until 30(34) sts rem. Work even in pat over these sts until length of armhole is same as on Back, ending at armhole edge.

SHOULDER: Bind off 8(9) sts at armhole edge every other row twice; then 7(8) sts every other row twice.

RIGHT FRONT: Work to correspond with Left Front, following first and all right-side rows from right front edge (marked center st on Chart) across to side line and reversing all shaping.

SLEEVES: Work same as for Left Front until the 16th row on Chart has been made. Keeping continuity of pat and working inc sts in pat, inc one st at each end of next row and every 1¼" thereafter—12 times in all—81(88) sts. Work even in pat until length is 17½(18)" from hemline, end with a p row.

Top Shaping: Keeping in pat, bind off 6 sts at beg of next 2 rows. Dec one st each end every other row until 23(24)

sts rem. Bind off 2 sts at beg of next 4 rows. Bind off rem sts.

FINISHING: Steam pieces very lightly from wrong side through a damp cloth. Sew shoulder seams. Turn all hems to wrong side at hemlines and stitch in place.

Front and Neck Band: Row 1: With right side facing, using crochet hook, sc evenly along right front edge, across back of neck and down left front edge, being careful to keep work flat. Ch 1, turn. **Rows 2-3:** Sc in each sc across. Ch 1, turn. **Row 4:** With pins mark the position of 4 buttonholes, evenly spaced along right front edge, with first pin 1" above hemline and last pin 1" below first dec of neck shaping. *Sc in each sc to within next pin, ch 3, sk 3 sc for buttonhole, sc in next sc; rep from * 3 more times; sc in each rem sc across. Ch 1, turn. **Row 5:** Sc in each sc and in each ch st across. Ch 1, turn. **Rows 6-7:** Rep Row 2. Break off and fasten. Sew side and sleeve seams. Sew in sleeves. Sew on buttons.

CAP: With No. 2 needles, cast on 128 sts. Work same as for Back until hemline has been made. Change to No. 3 needles and work in pat, repeating section marked on Chart across all sts for every right-side row until top of Chart is reached; then rep first through 9th rows on Chart, end with a p row. **Top Shaping:** Working without sequins work as follows: **Row 1:** * K 10, k 2 tog; rep from * across, ending with k 8 — 10 sts decreased. **Row 2:** P across. **Row 3:** *K 9, k 2 tog; rep from * across, ending with k 8. **Row 4:** P across. **Row 5:** K across, decreasing 10 sts evenly spaced across, having one st less before each dec than previous dec row. Rep last 2 rows alternately until 28 sts rem, ending with a p row. **Next Row:** *K 2 tog; rep from * across — 14 sts. **Next Row:** P across. Break off, leaving a 15" length of yarn. Thread this end into a darning needle and slip through rem sts. Pull tightly tog and sew back seam, matching rows. Turn hem to wrong side and stitch loosely in place.

SEQUIN JACKET

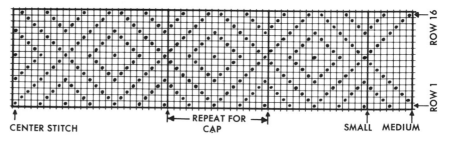

CENTER STITCH   ← REPEAT FOR CAP →   SMALL MEDIUM   ROW 16   ROW 1

⊞ SEQUIN

V NECK HALTER AND HAT

SIZES: Directions are for size 8. Changes for sizes 12, 14 and 16 are in parentheses.

MATERIALS: Bernat Dorlaine (40-gr balls): 2(2-3-3) balls of #6342 Silver/White for halter; 1 ball for hat. Knitting Needles, 1 pair Bernat–Aero, No. 4 OR SIZE TO OBTAIN GAUGE. Double-pointed Needles, 1 set Bernat-Aero, No. 4. Crochet Hook, Bernat-Aero, Size D or Size 3.00 mm).

GAUGE: Stockinette st — 13 sts = 2"; 8 rows = 1". Ribbing — 8 sts = 1"; 8 rows = 1".

FINISHED MEASUREMENTS: Width of back at underarm—14(14½-15¼-16)". Width of front at underarm—15(16-17-19½)".

HALTER-BACK: Cast on 97(103-109-115) sts. **Row 1:** K 1, *p 1, k 1; rep from * across row. **Row 2:** P 1, *k 1, p 1; rep from * across row. Rep these 2 rows for 4". Keeping continuity of ribbing throughout, inc one st each end of needle on next row and every 6th row thereafter 6 times more. Work even on 111(117-123-129) sts until piece measures 9½". **Shape Back:** Work in ribbing over 35 sts; join another ball of yarn and bind off center 41(47-53-59) sts, work to end of row. Working on both sides at once with separate strands at each center back edge bind off 4 sts every other row 6 times, and **At The Same Time,** dec 1 st at same edge every other row 6 times. Bind off rem 5 sts of each side.

FRONT: Work same as Back until piece measures 4", ending with Row 1. **Shape Front: Row 1 (wrong side):** P 2, work in ribbing to last 2 sts, p 2. **Row 2:** K 3, work in ribbing as established to last 3 sts, k 3. Continue in this manner to work one st more in st st (k 1 row, p 1 row) each end of needle Every Row until all

sts have been worked in st st, ending with a wrong-side row. **Shape Neck: Next Row:** K 47(50-53-56) sts, sl rem 50 (53-56-59) sts onto a st holder. Working on sts of Left Side Only, cast on 3 sts for overlap, turn—50(53-56-59) sts. **Row 1:** P 1, k 1, p to end of row. **Row 2:** K to last 4 sts, **k 2 tog, p 1, k 1—dec made at neck edge**. Keeping 2 sts at neck edge in p 1, k 1 ribbing and working all other sts in st st, continue to dec one st at neck edge in same manner as before every other row 32(34-36-38) times more, and **At The Same Time,** when piece measures same length as Back at side edge, Shape Side Edge as follows: **Row 1:** Bind off 6(6-7-8) sts, work to end of row. **Row 2:** Work to last 2 sts (arm edge), k 1, p 1. **Row 3:** K 1, p 1, k 2 tog through back loops, work to end of row. Rep last 2 rows 3(4-4-4) times. Then keeping 2 sts at arm edge in ribbing as established, continue to dec at neck edge in same manner as before until 7 sts rem. Work even on 7 sts until piece is desired length to center back of neck. Bind off. **Right Side:** Sl the 50(53-56-59) sts from holder onto needles. Join yarn at center front and finish to correspond to left side, reversing all shaping. To Dec At Arm Edge, work to last 4 sts, k 2 tog, p 1, k 1.

FINISHING: Sew side seams. Sew back of neck seam. Sew underlap in place. Steam seams.

Flower: Ch 6. Join with sl st to form a ring. **Rnd 1:** 12 sc in ring. **Rnd 2:** *Ch 4, sk next sc, sc in next sc; rep from * around—6 lps. **Rnd 3:** *In next ch-4 lp make sc, 3 dc and sc; rep from * around —6 petals. **Rnd 4:** *Ch 6, sk next 4 sts, sc in back lp of next sc; rep from * around. **Rnd 5:** *In next ch-6 lp make 1 sc, hdc, 4 dc, hdc and sc; rep from * around. **Rnd 6:** *Ch 8, sk next 7 sts, sc in back lp of next sc; rep from * around. **Rnd 7:** *In next ch-8 lp make sc, hdc, 7 dc, hdc and sc; rep from * around. **Rnd**

8: Sc in each st around. Join with sl st in next sc. Break off and fasten. **Center:** Ch 2. **Rnd 1:** Make 9 sc in 2nd ch from hook. **Rnd 2:** *Sk next sc, sc in each of next 2 sc; rep from * around. Sl st in first sc. Break off and fasten. Sew center to starting ring of flower. Sew flower to center front of halter at beg of neck shaping.

HAT: Using dp needles, cast on 128 sts. Divide sts evenly on 3 needles. Join, being careful not to twist sts. Work in rnds of k 1, p 1 ribbing for 6½". Now work in st st (k each rnd). **Shape Top: Dec Rnd 1:** *K 6, k 2 tog; rep from * around. K 4 rnds even. **Dec Rnd 2:** *K 5, k 2 tog; rep from * around. K 4 rnds even. **Dec Rnd 3:** *K 4, k 2 tog; rep from * around. K 4 rnds even. **Dec Rnd 4:** *K 3, k 2 tog; rep from * around. K 4 rnds even. **Dec Rnd 5:** *K 2, k 2 tog; rep from * around. K 4 rnds even. **Dec Rnd 6:** *K 1, k 2 tog; rep from * around. K 4 rnds even. **Dec Rnd 7:** K 2 tog around. Break off yarn, leaving an 8" end.

FINISHING: Using a darning needle, draw end through rem sts and pull up tightly. Fasten off. **Edging: Rnd 1:** With wrong side facing, sc evenly along lower edge of hat. **Rnd 2:** *Sc in each of next 2 sts, sl st in same st (picot); rep from * around. Join with sl st to first sc. Break off and fasten. **Flower: First Rnd of Petals:** Ch 6. Join with sl st to form a ring. **Rnd 1:** 12 sc in ring. **Rnd 2:** *Ch 5, make 2 tr in next sc, ch 5, sl st in next sc; rep from * around. Break off and fasten. Make 2 more rnds of petals in same way. Hold the 3 rnds of petals tog and sew rings tog. **Center:** Ch 2. **Rnd 1:** 6 sc in 2nd ch from hook. **Rnd 2:** Sc in each sc around. **Rnd 3:** (Sc in each of next 2 sc, 2 sc in next sc) twice. **Rnd 4:** Sc in each sc around. **Rnd 5:** Stuff with cotton, (sk next sc, sc in next sc) 4 times. Sl st in next sc. Break off and fasten. Sew to center of flower. Turn up brim. Sew flower to hat.

GARTER YOKE PULLOVER AND SLEEVELESS VEST

SIZES: Directions are for small (6-8) size. Changes for medium (10-12) and large (14) sizes are in parentheses.

MATERIALS: Columbia-Minerva Reverie (1 oz balls): **Pullover:** 7 (8-9) balls #2311 Blue. **Vest:** 5 (6-7) balls same color. Knitting Needles, No. 7 OR SIZE TO OBTAIN GAUGE. 4 buttons, ½" in diameter.

GAUGE: Stockinette st—5 sts = 1"; 6 rows = 1".

BLOCKING MEASUREMENTS: Pullover: Bust—31½ (34-36)". Width of back or front at underarm—15¾ (17-18)". Width of sleeve at upper arm—11 (11½-12)". **Vest:** Bust—32 (34½-36½)". Width of back at underarm—15¾ (17-18)". Width of each front below neck shaping, excluding band—7¾ (8½-9)".

PULLOVER

BACK: Cast on 78 (86-90) sts. Work in k 1, p 1 ribbing for 3". Work in st st (k 1 row, p 1 row) until length is 10 (10-11)" from beg, end with a p row.

ARMHOLES: Continuing in st st, bind off 4 (5-5) sts at beg of next 2 rows. Dec one st at each end every other row 7 (8-8) times—56 (60-64) sts. Now work in garter st (k each row) until length is 6½ (7-7½)" from first row of armholes.

SHOULDERS: Continuing in garter st, bind off 6 (7-8) sts at beg of next 2 rows. Place rem 44 (46-48) sts on a st holder.

FRONT: Work same as Back until length of armholes is 4½ (5-5½)".

NECK: Row 1: K 20 (22-24); place these sts just worked on a st holder; bind off next 16 sts; k rem sts. Working in garter st over the 20 (22-24) sts on needles only, at neck edge bind off 2 sts at beg of every other row until 10 sts rem; then dec one st at same edge every row until 6 (7-8) sts rem. Work even until length of armhole is same as on Back, ending at armhole edge. Bind off rem sts for shoulder. Place sts from holder

on a needle, attach yarn at neck edge and work to correspond with opposite side.

SLEEVES: Cast on 44 (46-48) sts. Work in k 1, p 1 ribbing for 2". Keeping continuity of ribbing, inc one st each end on next row and then again when piece measures 4". Work even in ribbing until total length is 5 (5-5½)". Now work in garter st throughout (k each row), increasing one st each end every 2" until there are 56 (58-60) sts. Work even until total length is 16½ (16½-17)".

Top Shaping: Continuing in garter st, bind off 4 (5-5) sts at beg of next 2 rows. Dec one st each end every 4th row 5 (7-8) times, then every other row 6 (4-4) times. Bind off 3 sts at beg of next 4 rows. Bind off rem sts.

FINISHING: To block, pin pieces to measurements on a padded surface; cover with a damp cloth and allow to dry; **do not press.** Sew left shoulder seam. **Neckband:** With right side facing, k sts on back holder, pick up and k evenly 68 (72-74) sts along front neck edge—112 (118-122) sts. Work in k 1, p 1 ribbing for 1". Bind off in ribbing. Sew right shoulder, side and sleeve seams. Sew in sleeves.

VEST

BACK: Cast on 78 (86-90) sts. Work in k 1, p 1 ribbing for 5". Work in st st (k 1 row, p 1 row) until total length is 12½ (12½-13)", end with a p row.

ARMHOLES: Continuing in st st, bind off 4 (5-5) sts at beg of next 2 rows, then bind off 3 sts at beg of following 2 rows. Dec one st each end every other row 2 (3-4) times—60 (64-66) sts. Work even in st st until length from first row of armholes is 2¼". For yoke, work in garter st (k each row) until length from first row of armhole is 7 (7½-8)".

SHOULDERS: Continuing in garter st, bind off 6 (7-7) sts at beg of next 4 rows. Bind off rem 36 (36-38) sts.

LEFT FRONT: Cast on 38 (42-44) sts. Work same as Back until total length is 10 (10-10½)"; end with a p row.

NECK: Next Row: K across to within last 2 sts, **k 2 tog—dec made at front edge.** Dec one st at front edge every 4th row until total length is 12½ (12½-13)", end with a p row.

ARMHOLE: At side edge, bind off 4 (5-5) sts at beg of next k row; while continuing decs at front edge every 4th row as before, **at the same time—at** armhole edge bind off 3 sts at beg of next k row, then dec one st every other row 2 (3-4) times. Keeping armhole edge straight and starting garter st yoke to correspond with Back, continue to dec one st at front edge every 4th row until 12 (14-14) sts rem. Work even until length of armhole is same as on Back; end at armhole edge.

SHOULDER: Bind off 6 (7-7) sts at beg of next row. K 1 row. Bind off rem sts.

RIGHT FRONT: Work to correspond with Left Front, reversing shaping.

Pocket (Make 2): Cast on 18 sts. Work in st st for 2½". Work in k 1, p 1 ribbing for 5 rows. Bind off in ribbing.

FINISHING: To block, pin pieces to measurements on a padded surface; cover with a damp cloth and allow to dry; **do not press.** Sew side and shoulder seams. **Front and Neck Band:** Start at right front lower edge, cast on 8 sts. Work in k 1, p 1 ribbing for 1½". **Buttonhole Row:** K 1, p 1, k 1, bind off 2 sts, k 1, p 1. **Next Row:** Work first 3 sts in ribbing, cast on 2 sts, complete row. Work in k 1, p 1 ribbing, making a buttonhole every 2½" until 4 buttonholes in all have been made. Continue in ribbing until band fits (slightly stretched) along right front, back of neck and left front edges. Bind off. Sew band in place, with buttonholes on right front edge. Sew on buttons. Sew one pocket to center of each front, with lower edge at top of ribbing.

SIZES: Directions are for small (6-8) size. Changes for medium (10-12) and large (14) sizes are in parentheses.

MATERIALS: Columbia-Minerva Nantuk Sport Yarn (2 oz skn): **Cardigan:** 7 (8–9) skns #6077 Pink. **Tank Top:** 2 (2–3) skns same color. Knitting Needles, No. 6 OR SIZE TO OBTAIN GAUGE. Crochet Hook, Size E. 8 small button molds.

GAUGE: Ribbing—7 sts = 1"; 6 rows = 1".

BLOCKING MEASUREMENTS: Cardigan: Bust—32 (34-36)". Width of back at underarm—16 (17-18)". Width of each front at underarm—8½ (9-9½)". Width of sleeve at upper arm—12 (12½-13)". **Tank Top:** To fit Bust Size 30-31½ (32½-34, 36)".

CARDIGAN

BACK: Start at lower edge, cast on 112 (120-128) sts. Work in k 2, p 2 ribbing throughout back. Work in ribbing until total length is 18".

ARMHOLES: Keeping continuity of ribbing, bind off 5 (5-6) sts at beg of next 2 rows. Dec one st at each end every other row until 94 (102-106) sts rem. Work even until armholes measure 7 (7½-8)".

SHOULDERS: Keeping continuity of ribbing, bind off 8 (9-10) sts at beg of next 4 rows. Place rem 62 (66-66) sts on a st holder for neckband.

LEFT FRONT: Start at lower edge, cast on 61 (65-69) sts. **Row 1:** Work in k 2, p 2 ribbing across to within last 9 sts, **k 1 (p 1, k 1) 4 times—front band. Row 2:** P 1, (k 1, p 1) 4 times for front band; complete row in k 2, p 2 ribbing. Rep Rows 1-2 alternately until total length is 18", end at side edge.

ARMHOLE: Bind off 5 (5-6) sts at beg of row; complete row, keeping in ribbing as established. Keeping continuity of ribbing, dec one st at armhole edge every other row 4 (4-5) times. If necessary, work even over rem 52 (56-58) sts until armhole measures 2"; end at front edge.

NECK: Work first 9 sts as before; place these sts on a safety pin, bind off 3 sts; complete row. Keeping in ribbing, bind off 3 sts at neck edge every other row until 16 (20-22) sts rem; then bind off 0 (2-2) sts once. Work even over 16 (18-20) sts until length of armhole is same as on back, ending at armhole edge.
Shoulder: Row 1: At armhole edge, bind off 8 (9-10) sts. **Row 2:** Work even. Bind off. With pins, mark the position of 7 buttons, evenly spaced along front band, having first pin 2" above lower edge and last pin 2" below neck edge.

The 8th button will be placed on neckband. **To make a buttonhole on right front—starting at front edge work in ribbing over first 3 sts, bind off next 3 sts; complete row. On next row, cast on 3 sts over the bound-off sts.**

RIGHT FRONT: Making buttonholes as directed, opposite pins on Left Front, work to correspond with Left Front, reversing all shaping.

SLEEVES: Cast on 56 (60-64) sts. Work in k 2, p 2 ribbing for 2". Keeping continuity of ribbing, inc one st each end on next row and every 6th row thereafter until there are 84 (88-94) sts. Work even until total length is 17 (17-18)".
Top Shaping: Keeping in ribbing, bind off 5 (5-6) sts at beg of next 2 rows. Dec one st at each end every row until 20 sts rem. Bind off 2 sts at beg of next 4 rows. Bind off in ribbing rem sts.
Button (Make 8): With crochet hook, ch 5. Join with sl st to form a ring. **Rnd 1:** 8 sc in ring. Do not join. **Rnd 2:** Working in back lp only of each sc, sc in 8 sc. **Rnd 3:** Insert button mold and work same as for last rnd. **Rnd 4:** (Sk next sc, sc in next sc) 4 times. Leaving a 6" length, break off. Using this end of yarn, sew sts of last rnd tog.

FINISHING: To block, pin pieces to measurements on a padded surface; cover with a damp cloth and allow to dry; **do not press.** Sew side, shoulder and sleeve seams. **Neckband:** With right side facing, place the 9 sts from right front safety pin on a needle, attach yarn and pick up and k 46 (48-50) sts evenly along right front neck edge to shoulder seam, k across sts on back holder, decreasing 5 sts evenly spaced across; pick up and k 46 (48-50) sts along left front neck edge to next safety pin, work in ribbing as established on front band across sts on safety pin—167 (175-179) sts. **Row 1 (wrong side):** Work in ribbing as established on front band over first 9 sts and continue in k 1, p 1 ribbing across all sts. Making a buttonhole in line with previous buttonholes when neckband measures ½", continue in ribbing as established for 1", end with a wrong-side row. Bind off tightly in ribbing. Sew in sleeves. Sew on buttons.

TANK TOP

BACK: Cast on 84 (92-100) sts. Work in k 2, p 2 ribbing for 11 (11½-12)".

ARMHOLES: Rows 1-2: Keeping continuity of ribbing bind off 10 (12-12) sts at beg of each of 2 rows—64 (68-76) sts. **Row 3:** (K 1, p 1) 3 times for armhole band; work in ribbing as established on previous rows across to within last 6

sts; for other armhole band (p 1, k 1) 3 times. **Rows 4-5:** Rep last row. **Row 6:** (K 1, p 1) 3 times; **k 2 tog—dec made inside armhole band;** work across to within last 8 sts, p 2 tog (p 1, k 1) 3 times—dec made at each end inside armhole band. Rep last 4 rows once more.

NECK: Row 1: (K 1, p 1) 3 times; work in ribbing as before over next 10 (10-12) sts, (p 1, k 1) 3 times for neck band. Place these 22 (22-24) sts just worked on a st holder. Bind off in ribbing next 16 (20-24) sts; p next st (k 1, p 1) twice; work as before across next 10 (10-12) sts, (p 1, k 1) 3 times. Keeping first and last 6 sts in k 1, p 1 ribbing for bands, work even over 22 (22-24) sts on needle only for 3 rows; dec one st inside band at each end of next row and every 4th row thereafter until 16 sts rem. Work in k 1, p 1 ribbing across all sts until length of armhole is same as on back. Bind off in ribbing. Place sts from holder on a needle; attach yarn at neck edge and work to correspond with opposite side.

FRONT: Work same as Back until total length is 6". **Next Row (right side):** (K 2, p 2) twice; p 29 (33-37), **k 2, (p 2, k 2) twice—center panel;** p 29 (33-37), (k 2, p 2) twice. **Next Row:** (K 2, p 2) twice; k 29 (33-37), p 2, (k 2, p 2) twice; k 29 (33-37), (k 2, p 2) twice. Rep last 2 rows until length is 11 (11½-12)" from beg; end with a wrong-side row.

ARMHOLES: Rows 1-2: Keeping center panel in ribbing as established and all other sts in reverse st st (p on right side, k on wrong side), bind off 10 (12-12) sts at beg of 2 rows. **Row 3:** (K 1, p 1) 3 times for armhole band; work across as before to within last 6 sts, (p 1, k 1) 3 times. **Rows 4-5:** Rep last row. **Row 6:** Dec one st inside armhole band at each end. Rep last 4 rows once.

NECK: (K 1, p 1) 3 times; p 12 (14-18), (k 1, p 1) 3 times for neck band. Place these sts on a st holder. Bind off in ribbing next 12 sts, p next st, (k 1, p 1), twice; p to last 6 sts, (p 1, k 1) 3 times—24 (26-30) sts. Keeping first and last 6 sts in k 1, p 1 ribbing, and other sts in reverse st st, work 3 rows even; dec one st inside band at each end on next row and every 4th row thereafter until 16 sts rem. Work in k 1, p 1 ribbing over all sts until armhole is same length as on Back. Bind off in ribbing. Work over sts on holder to correspond with opposite side.

FINISHING: To block, pin pieces to measurements on a padded surface; cover with a damp cloth and allow to dry; **do not press.** Sew side and shoulder seams.

HIGH POCKET RIBBED PULLOVER

SIZES: Directions are for size 10. Changes for sizes 12 and 14 are in parentheses.

MATERIALS: Bear Brand's Rose Pink Winsom (2-oz sk), 5 (5,6) skeins. Knitting Needles, 1 pair each No. 4 and No. 7 OR SIZE TO OBTAIN GAUGE.

GAUGE: Ribbing On No. 7 needles, 21 sts = 4"; 7 rows = 1".

BLOCKING MEASUREMENTS: Bust—36 (38,40)". Width of back or front at underarm—18 (19,20)"; width of sleeve at upperarm—12½ (13,13)".

BACK: With No. 4 needles, cast on 94 (98, 102) sts. **Row 1** (wrong side): P 2, * k 2, p 2. Rep from * to end. **Row 2:** K 2, * p 2, k 2. Rep from * to end. Rep these 2 rows for 5". Change to No. 7 needles. Continue ribbing until 9½" from beg or desired length to underarm, end on right side row. Mark last row.

ARMHOLES: Bind off 5 sts in ribbing at beg of next 2 rows. Keep to pat, dec 1 st each end every other row 6 times—72 (76,80) sts. Continue ribbing until 7¼ (7½,7¾)" above underarm marker, end right side row.

SHOULDERS: Bind off 5 sts at beg of next 6 rows; 4 (6,8) sts at beg of next 2 rows—34 sts. Bind off.

FRONT: Work same as back until 5¼ (5½,-5¾)" above underarm marker, end wrong side row—72 (76,80) sts.

DIVIDE FOR NECK: Work 27 (29,31) sts and place on holder for left side; bind off 18 sts for neck; work rem 27 (29,31) sts for right side. Continue on sts of right side, dec 1 st at neck edge every row 6 times; every other row twice, shaping shoulder as for left shoulder of back when armhole is same length as back. Beg at armhole edge, pick up sts of left side on No. 7 needles. Join yarn at neck edge and finish to correspond to right side.

SLEEVES: With No. 4 needles, cast on 42 (46,46) sts. Work ribbing as for back for 2½" end wrong side row. Change to No. 7 needles. Keep to pat and inc 1 st each end of next row, then every 6th row 6 times; every 8th row 5 times—66 (70,70) sts. Work even until 15" from beg or desired length to underarm, end right side row.

TOP SHAPING: Bind off 5 sts at beg of next 2 rows. Dec 1 st each end every other row 15 (16,16) times. Bind off 2 sts at beg of next 4 rows. Bind off rem 18 (20,20) sts.

POCKETS—(Make 2): With No. 7 needles, cast on 26 sts. Work ribbing as for back until 3" from beg. Bind off loosely in ribbing.
Steam press lightly. Sew shoulder seams, matching ribs. Sew underarm and sleeve seams sewing 1 st in from edges. Sew in sleeves, sewing 1 st in from armhole edge. Sew pockets to front as in photo.

MULTI-COLOR STRIPED PULLOVER

SIZES: Directions are for size 8. Changes for sizes 10, 12 and 14 are in parentheses.

MATERIALS: Bucilla Wool & Shetland Wool (2-oz skeins), Electra Blue (Color A), 1 (2, 2, 2) skeins. Green Apple (Color B), Pumpkin (Color C), Orange (Color D), Peach Chiffon (Color E), Bright Navy (Color F), Chinese Blue (Color G), Lavender (Color H), Scarlet (Color I), Rosy Pink (Color J), 1 skein each. Knitting needles; 1 pair each of No. 4 and No. 6 OR SIZE TO OBTAIN GAUGE. 7″ neck or skirt zipper.

GAUGE: 6 sts = 1″; 7 rows = 1″.

BLOCKING MEASUREMENTS: Bust—34 (36,38,39)″. Width of back or front at underarm—17 (18, 19, 19½)″, width of sleeves at upperarm—12½ (12¾, 13¼, 13¾)″.

PATTERN: Work in stockinette st (k on right side, p on wrong side) for 8 rows with each color, in color sequence A, B, C, D, E, F, G, H, I, J, A, B, C, D and E. **Pattern Note:** When changing colors leave an 8″ strand for sewing.

BACK: With No. 4 needles, and A cast on 76 (80, 84, 88) sts loosely. Work in stockinette st starting with a p row for 6 rows for hem facing, end with k row. K next row for turning ridge. Change to No. 6 needles. **Next Row** (right side): Knit. Work in stockinette st with A until 8 rows above turning ridge. Break A, join B. Continue in pat until 2 rows of C are completed. **Next Row** (Inc Row): K 1 st, inc 1 st in next st, k to within 2 sts of end, inc 1 st in next st, k 1. Continue in pat, until 2 rows of E are completed. **Next Row:** Rep inc row. Continue in pat, inc in 3rd row of F, G and H

stripes. Work even until 6 rows of H are completed (about 9″ above turning ridge) end p row—86 (90, 94, 98) sts.

ARMHOLES: Bind off 4 (4, 5, 5) sts at beg of next 2 rows. **Next Row:** Break H, join I. K 1, sl 1, k 1, psso, knit to within 3 sts of end, k 2 tog, k 1. Keeping to pat, dec 1 st each end every other row 3 (3, 3, 4) times—70 (74, 76, 78) sts. Work even until 4 (4, 8, 8) rows of D stripe completed, about 6¾ (6¾, 7¼, 7¼)″ above underarm, end with p row.

SHOULDER AND NECK SHAPING: Keeping to pat, bind off 7 (8, 8, 8) sts at beg of next 4 rows, then bind off 8 (8, 8, 9) sts at beg of next 2 rows—26 (26, 28, 28) sts rem for neck.

NECKBAND: With E work even on 26 (26, 28, 28) sts for 4 rows, end with p row. Change to No. 4 needles. **Next Row** (right side): Purl for turning ridge. With E, work 4 rows even. Bind off loosely.

FRONT: Work same as for back until 3 rows are completed in 2nd stripe of A, end with k row.

NECK AND LEFT SHOULDER: Next Row: P 28 (30, 31, 32) sts for right shoulder and place on holder, p next 14 sts and place on holder for neck, p rem 28 (30, 31, 32) sts for left shoulder. Keeping to pat, work left shoulder in stockinette st, dec 1 st at neck edge every row 4 (4, 5, 5) times, then dec 1 st at neck edge every other row twice. Work even in pat until 4 (4, 8, 8) rows of D stripe are completed, end with p row. Keeping to pat, bind off 7 (8, 8, 8) sts at armhole edge twice,

then bind off 8 (8, 8, 9) sts at armhole edge once.

RIGHT SHOULDER: Sl 28 (30, 31, 32) sts from holder to No. 6 needle. With right side facing you, join yarn at neck edge and work corresponding to left shoulder.

SLEEVES: Note: Color sequence for sleeves starts with E, F, G, H, I, J, A, B, C, D, etc. With No. 4 needles and E cast on 30 (32, 34, 36) sts. Work as for back keeping to pat until 14 rows above turning ridge, end with p row. Inc 1 st each end of next row, then every 6th row, 15 times more—62 (64, 66, 68) sts. Work even for 5 rows ending with 6th row of 2nd stripe of H (approximately 15¾″) for bracelet length sleeves.

TOP SHAPING: Bind off 4 (4, 5, 5) sts at beg of next 2 rows. Keeping to pat, dec 1 st each end every other row 16 (17, 18, 19) times, then every row 5 (5, 4, 4) times. Bind off rem 12 sts.

FRONT NECKBAND: From right side, with No. 6 needles and E, beg at left shoulder, pick up and k 26 (26, 28, 28) sts on left neck edge, k 14 sts from holder, pick up and k 26 (26, 28, 28) sts on right shoulder—66 (66, 70, 70) sts. Work st st for 3 rows even, end with p row. Change to No. 4 needles, p next row for turning ridge. With E work even in st st for 9 rows. Bind off loosely.

FINISHING: Block pieces to measurements. Sew shoulder, neckband, sleeve and side seams matching stripes and leaving left side seam open 7″ above turning ridge. Sew in sleeves. Turn hems and sew to wrong side. Sew zipper in left side with opening at lower edge.

SIZES: Instructions are for petite size. Changes for small, medium and large are in parentheses.

MATERIALS: Spinnerin Sport Yarn (2-oz ball): 5 (5–6–6) balls White (MC) and 1 ball Hot Pink (CC) for embroidery of heart. Knitting Needles Nos. 5 and 3. Circular Needle, No. 3 OR SIZE TO OBTAIN GAUGE. Crochet Hook, Size F.

GAUGE: 6 sts = 1"; 8 rows = 1".

BLOCKING MEASUREMENTS: Bust— 31 (32-33-35)". Width of back or front at underarm—15½ (16-16½-17½)". Width of sleeve at upper arm—11 (11½-11¾-12)".

BACK: Start at lower edge with MC and No. 3 needles, cast on 82 (86-90-94) sts. Work in k 1, p 1 ribbing for 2". Change to No. 5 needles and work in stockinette st (k 1 row, p 1 row) for 1". Inc one st each side of next row and every 2" thereafter 4 more times. Work even (no more incs) over 92 (96-100-104) sts to 12" from beg, or desired length to underarm.

ARMHOLES: Bind off 5 sts at beg of next 2 rows. Dec one st each side every other row 3 (4-4-5) times. Work over 76 (78-82-84) sts until armholes measure 4½ (4½-5-5)".

NECK AND SHOULDERS: Work 20 (21-23-24) sts; place center 36 sts on a stitch holder; join second ball of yarn and with second strand, complete row. Working each side with separate ball of yarn, dec one st at each neck edge every row 10 times. **At The Same Time,** when armholes measure 5¾ (6-6½-7)", from each armhole edge bind off 3 (3-4-4) sts every other row twice, 4 (5-5-6) sts once.

FRONT: Work same as Back until armhole shaping has been completed.

NECK AND SHOULDERS: Work 31 (32-34-35) sts; place center 14 sts on a stitch holder; join second ball of yarn and with this strand complete row. Working each side with separate ball of yarn, bind off 2 sts at each neck edge every other row 5 times. Dec one st at each neck edge every other row 11 times. Work even until armholes are same length as on Back. Shape shoulders same as for Back.

SLEEVES: With No. 3 needles and MC, cast on 48 (50-52-54) sts. Work in k 1, p 1 ribbing for 2". Change to No. 5 needles and work in stockinette st, inc one st each side every 12th row 9 times. Work over 66 (68-70-72) sts until length is 17" from beg, or desired length to underarm.

Top Shaping: Bind off 5 sts at beg of next 2 rows. Dec one st each side every other row 15 (16-17-18) times. Bind off 2 sts at beg of next 4 rows. Bind off rem 18 sts.

FINISHING: Block pieces to measurements. Sew side, shoulder and sleeve seams. Sew in sleeves. **Neckband:** With circular needle from right side, starting at right shoulder seam, pick up and k 68 sts along back of neck, including sts on holder; pick up and k 40 sts along left front neck edge to front holder, k the 14 sts on holder, pick up and k 40 sts along right front neck edge—162 sts. Work in rnds of k 1, p 1 ribbing for 4 rnds. Bind off in ribbing.

EMBROIDERY: There are actually two complete hearts which should appear as one when your arm is resting next to your body. See photo for placement. Mark position of one heart on right side of sweater body and the other on right sleeve, centering each over a seam line so that half is on front of sweater and half on back. Following chart, baste outline of each heart in position on sweater and with tapestry needle and CC, embroider in duplicate st. If desired, embroider hearts on ready-made knee socks as for sweater, using small heart chart.

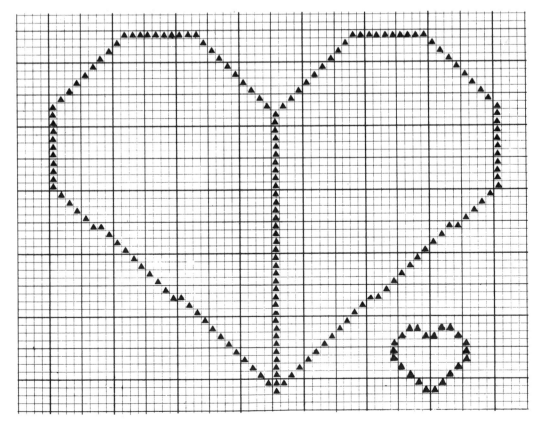

FRINGED MOHAIR DRESS OR SKIRT

NOTE: Photograph shows strapless mid-calf dress which may also be worn as a long skirt.

SIZE: Directions are for skirt size 8–10. Changes for 12–14 are in parentheses. Shawl is one size for all.

MATERIALS: Reynolds Mohair No. 1, 6 balls for skirt; 5 balls for shawl. 1 yard ½" elastic for skirt. Knitting Needle, 29" circular needle No. 13. Aluminum crochet hook size G. 2½" × 8" cardboard to make fringe.

GAUGE: 7 sts = 3"; 18 rows or rnds (9 ridges—1 pat) = 3¼" (unblocked). **Test Piece:** Cast on 14 sts. Work in pat for shawl for 18 rows. Piece should measure 6" wide, 3¼" long. If too small, try larger needles; if too large, try smaller needles, until correct gauge is obtained.

PATTERN FOR SHAWL: Rows 1–16: Work in garter st (k each row)—8 ridges. **Row 17** (mark row right side): Knit. **Row 18:** Wind yarn around 2½" cardboard from right to left 58 times for first loop fringe row, keeping loops separated side by side. If desired transfer loops to a long dp needle.

JOIN LOOP FRINGE: Inc 1 st in first st on needle; holding cardboard (or dp needle) on right side of work (behind this row) and beg at right edge, * insert left-hand needle under 1 loop on cardboard (or dp needle), k the loop together with 1 st from work. Repeat from * to last st on row, inc 1 st in last st. Repeat these 18 rows for pat; winding yarn around cardboard 76 times for row 36; 94 times for row 54; 100 times for row 72; 106 times for row 90; 112 times for row 108.

SHAWL: Cast on loosely 44 sts. **Rows 1–18:**

Working in pat, inc 1 st each end every other row 9 times—58 fringe, 62 sts on row 18 (row should measure 26½" wide). **Rows 19–36:** Repeat rows 1–18 of shawl—76 fringe, 80 sts on row 36. **Rows 37–54:** Repeat rows 1–18 of shawl—94 fringe, 98 sts on row 54. **Rows 55–72:** Working in pat, inc 1 st each end every 6th row 3 times—100 fringe, 104 sts on row 72. **Rows 73–90:** Repeat rows 55–72 of shawl—106 fringe, 110 sts on row 90. **Rows 91–108:** Repeat rows 55–72 of shawl—112 fringe, 116 sts on row 108. Sixth loop fringe row completed. Work in garter st for 3 rows. Bind off loosely.

FINISHING: From right side, work 1 row sc around entire edge of shawl, keeping edge flat and working 3 sc in each corner at top edge. Join rnd with slip st, end off. Beg at top left edge and right side, work 1 row reverse sc (work from left to right) across top edge of shawl. End off. Run in ends on wrong side. Steam-press lightly on wrong side to desired width and length.

FRINGE: Cut 5 strands 8" long. Fold these 5 strands in half to form loop. Insert hook from wrong to right side in a st on edge of shawl, draw ends through loop and pull up tight. Knot fringe in every other st around entire curved edge of stole.

MID-CALF DRESS

Actual Knitted Measurements: Width around bottom—60 (63)"; around hips—36 (39)"; around waistline before waistband—30 (33)". Length of skirt 30" (4" allowance for stretch).

PATTERN FOR SKIRT: Rnds 1–16: Work in garter st (k 1 rnd, p 1 rnd) alternately. **Rnd 17:** Wind yarn around 2½" cardboard, from right to left as many times as sts on needle,

for example 133 (140) times after first dec rnd. Keep loops separated side by side. If desired transfer loops on a long dp needle. **JOIN LOOP FRINGE:** Holding cardboard (or dp needle) on right side of work (in front of this rnd) and beg at right edge, * insert right-hand needle under 1 loop on cardboard (or dp needle) and 1 loop on needle and k them off tog as 1 st. Repeat from * to end of rnd. **Rnd 18:** P 1 rnd. Repeat these 18 rnds for pat.

SKIRT: Beg at lower edge, with circular needle, cast on loosely 140 (147) sts. **Rnds 1–11:** Join and work rnds 1–11 of pat. **Rnd 12** (First Dec Rnd): * P 18 (19) sts, p 2 tog. Repeat from * around—133 (140) sts. **Rnds 13–18:** Continue in pat for skirt. Repeat rnds 1–18 of skirt hereafter, making decs on 12th rnd of each pat stripe 7 more times as follows: **2nd Dec Rnd:** * P 17 (18) sts, p 2 tog. Repeat from * around—126 (133) sts. **3rd Dec Rnd:** * P 16 (17) sts, p 2 tog. Repeat from * around—119 (126) sts. **4th Dec Rnd:** * P 15 (16) sts, p 2 tog. Repeat from * around —112 (119) sts. **5th Dec Rnd:** * P 14 (15) sts, p 2 tog. Repeat from * around—105 (112) sts. **6th Dec Rnd:** * P 13 (14) sts, p 2 tog. Repeat from * around—98 (105) sts. **7th Dec Rnd:** * P 12 (13) sts, p 2 tog. Repeat from * around—91 (98) sts. **8th Dec Rnd:** * P 11 (12) sts, p 2 tog. Repeat from * around —84 (91) sts. Work in garter st for 4 more rnds. Work in k 1, p 1 ribbing for 1¼" for casing.

FINISHING: Steam press lightly on wrong side to desired width and length. **Casing:** Turn down and sew 1¼" ribbing at top edge to wrong side for casing leaving a small opening; draw elastic through to desired fit. Sew opening.

SIZES: Directions are for petite size. Changes for small, medium and large sizes are in parentheses.

MATERIALS: Bernat Berella Sportspun, 100% acrylic (2-oz ball): 5 (5–6–6) balls of #2810 Brown (A); 1 ball each of #2835 Paiute Red (B), #2837 Rose Heather (C) and #2890 Violet (D). About 20 to 25 yds each of #2809 Old Gold (E), #2832 Coral (F), #2889 Shannon Green (G) and #2887 Frosty Aqua (H) or colors as desired. Knitting Needles, 1 pair each of Nos. 5 and 7 OR SIZE TO OBTAIN GAUGE.

GAUGE: 11 sts = 2"; 7 rows = 1".

MEASUREMENTS: Width of back and front at underarms — 15½ (16½-17½-18½)"; sleeves at upperarm—10¾ (11¼-12-13)".

BACK: With No. 5 needles and A cast on 86 (90-96-102) sts. K 1, p 1 in ribbing for 5". Change to No. 7 needles. Work in st st (k 1 row, p 1 row) until 11" from beg.

Armholes: Bind off 5 (5-6-7) sts at beg of next 2 rows. Dec 1 st each side every other row 5 (6-6-7) times—66 (68-72-74) sts. Work even until 6¾ (7-7½-8)" above underarms.

SHOULDERS: Bind off 7 (7-8-8) sts at beg of next 4 rows; 7 (8-7-8) sts at beg of next 2 rows. Place rem 24 (24-26-26) sts on a holder.

FRONT: Work ribbing same as back. Change to No. 7 needles. Work 4 rows st st.

NOTE: Wind bobbins of colors. Do not carry colors more than the width of medallions or blocks. Carry only color A completely across a row. When changing colors bring new color from under dropped color to avoid a hole in work.

On all k rows, read chart from right to left in the following manner: Work from 86 (90-96-102) sts to A; repeat pat from B to 86 (90-96-102) sts. On all p rows, read chart from left to right in the following manner: Work from 86 (90-96-102) sts to B; repeat pat from A to 86 (90-96-102) sts.

Work even following chart until same length as back to underarm. Shape arm-

holes same as back. **At Same Time,** when 1½" above underarms, place center 18 (18-20-20) sts on a holder. Working on sts of one side, completing armhole decs and dec 1 st at neck edge every other row 3 times, work a medallion with color C 8 rows above last medallion; a block in colors E and H and another medallion in color B spaced 8 rows apart. Center the medallions on the sts of the front. Continue until armhole measures same as back.

SHOULDER: At armhole edge bind off 7 (7-8-8) sts twice; 7 (8-7-8) sts once. Join yarn at neck edge and work other side to correspond.

SLEEVES: With No. 5 needles and A cast on 40 (42-44-46) sts. K 1, p 1 in ribbing for 3". Change to No. 7 needles.

Work in st st and inc 1 st each side every 6th row 9 (10-11-12) times —58 (62-66-70) sts. Work even until sleeve measures 17".

SHAPING: Bind off 5 (5-6-7) sts at beg of next 2 rows. Dec 1 st each side every other row 10 (11-12-13) times. Bind off 3 sts at beg of next 4 rows. Bind off rem sts.

NECKBAND: Seam left shoulder. On right side with No. 5 needles, pick up and k about 112 (116-120-124) sts all around neck edge including sts on holders. K 1, p 1 in ribbing for 1". Bind off in ribbing.

FINISHING: Seam right shoulder joining neckband edges. Sew side and sleeve seams. Sew in sleeves. Block to measurements worked.

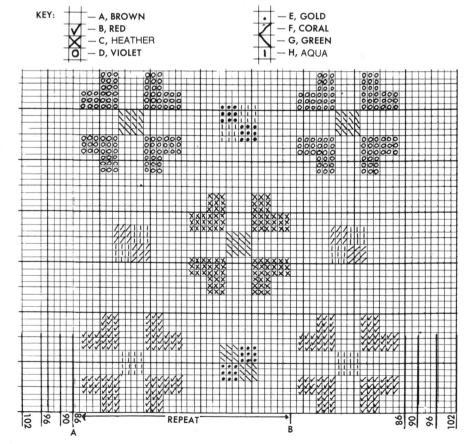

KEY:
- □ — A, BROWN
- ✓ — B, RED
- ⊠ — C, HEATHER
- ⊙ — D, VIOLET
- • — E, GOLD
- ◁ — F, CORAL
- ╱ — G, GREEN
- ‖ — H, AQUA

RAINBOW-STRIPED PULLOVER AND MATCHING HAT

SIZES: Directions for sweater are for size 8. Changes for sizes 10, 12 and 14 are in parentheses. Hat will fit all sizes.

MATERIALS: Coats and Clark's Red Heart "Wintuk"†, 4 ply (4 oz "Tangleproof" Pull-out Skeins): **For Sweater** 10 (11–12–13) ozs of #12 Black and 1 oz each of #588 Amethyst, #815 Brigantine Blue, #669 Mint Julep, #245 Orange, #253 Tangerine and #902 Jockey Red. **For Hat:** ½ oz each of Black and all colors needed for sweater. Knitting Needles, No. 8 OR SIZE TO OBTAIN GAUGE. Crochet Hook, Size I.

GAUGE: Stockinette st, 9 sts = 2"; 6 rows = 1". 7 sc = 2"; 4 rnds = 1".

BLOCKING MEASUREMENTS: Bust—32½ (33½–35–37)". Width of back or front at underarm—17¼ (17¾–18½–19½)". Width of sleeve at upper arm—12 (12½–13–13½)"

SWEATER—BACK: Starting at inner edge of hem with Black, cast on 77 (79–83–87) sts. Work in stockinette st (k 1 row, p 1 row) for 1" for hem, end with a k row. **Next Row:** K across for turning ridge. Starting with a k row, work in stockinette st for 8 rows. Continuing in stockinette st, dec. one st both ends of next row and every 6th row thereafter 6 times in all. Work even over rem 65 (67–71–75) sts until length is 7½" from turning ridge. Inc one st both ends of next row and every 4th row thereafter 4 times in all. Work even over 73 (75–79–83) until length from turning ridge is 10½ (10½–11–11)", ending with a p row. Break off Black; attach Amethyst. With Amethyst, work 6 rows even in stockinette st. Break off Amethyst; attach Blue. With Blue, work 6 rows even. Break off Blue; attach Green. With Green, work 6 rows even. Break off Green; attach Orange. With Orange, work 6 rows even. Break off Orange; attach Tangerine. With Tangerine, work 4 rows even.

ARMHOLES: With Tangerine, bind off 4 (4–5–5) sts at beg of next 2 rows. Break off

Tangerine; attach Red. With Red, dec one st both ends of next row and every other row 3 times in all, end with a p row—59 (61–63–67) sts. Break off Red; attach Black. **For Size 14 Only:** With Black, dec one st both ends of next row. **For All Sizes:** With Black, work even over rem 59 (61–63–65) sts until length is 5½ (6–6½–7)" from first row of armholes, end with a p row.

NECK AND SHOULDERS: Row 1: K 38 (39–41–42), place the sts just worked on a st holder, k rem 21 (22–22–23) sts. Work over set of sts on needle only. **Row 2:** Purl. **Row 3:** Bind off 3 sts—neck edge; complete row. **Row 4:** Purl. **Row 5:** Bind off 2 sts; complete row. **Row 6:** At side edge, bind off 4 (4–4–5) sts; complete row. Rep Rows 5, 6 and 5. Bind off 4 (5–5–4) sts. Leaving the center 17 (17–19–19) sts on st holder, slip rem 21 (22–22–23) sts onto a needle, attach yarn at neck edge and complete to correspond with opposite side, reversing shapings. **Neck Facing:** With right side facing and Black, start at right shoulder pick up and k 9 sts along right neck edge, k the 17 (17–19–19) sts on st holder, pick up and k 9 sts along left neck edge—35 (35–37–37) sts. K 1 row for turning ridge. **Next 5 rows:** Start with a k row, work in stockinette st, inc one st both ends of next row and every other row 3 times in all—41 (41–43–43) sts. Bind off.

FRONT: Work same as Back.

SLEEVES: Start at inner edge of hem with Black, cast on 32 (34–37–39) sts. Work in stockinette st for 1" for hem, end with a k row. **Next Row:** K across for turning ridge. Start with a k row, continue in stockinette st throughout, inc one st both ends of every 8th row 11 times in all. Work even in stockinette st over 54 (56–59–61) sts until length from turning ridge is 16½ (17–17–17½)", end with a p row.

TOP SHAPING: Bind off 4 (4–5–5) sts at beg of next 2 rows. Dec one st both ends of every other row until 22 (22–21–21) remain.

Bind off 2 sts at beg of next 4 rows. Bind off rem 14 (14–13–13) sts.

FINISHING: Block pieces to measurements. Sew side, shoulder and sleeve seams. Sew in sleeves. Turn all hems and neck facing to wrong side at turning ridges and stitch in place.

HAT—Crown: Start at center top with Black and crochet hook, ch 4. Join with sl st to form ring. **Rnd 1:** Make 6 sc in ring. Join with sl st to first sc. **Rnd 2:** Ch 1, 2 sc in same sc as joining, 2 sc in each sc around. Join to first sc—12 sc. **Rnd 3:** Ch 1, sc in same sc as joining, * 2 sc in next sc—**inc made;** sc in next sc: rep from * around, end with 2 sc in last sc. Join—6 sc increased. **Rnd 4:** Ch 1, sc in same sc as joining, increasing 6 sc evenly spaced around, sc in each sc. Join—24 sc. **Rnds 5–10:** Being careful not to have incs fall directly over incs of previous rnd, rep 4th rnd 6 times—60 sc. At end of last rnd, break off and fasten. Attach Red to same sc as joining. **Rnd 11:** With Red, ch 1, sc in same sc as joining, sc in each sc around. Join. **Next 3 Rnds:** Rep last rnd. At end of last rnd, break off and fasten. Attach Tangerine to same sc as joining. **Next 4 Rnds:** With Tangerine, work same as for last 4 rnds. Break off and fasten. Continuing to work as for last 4 rnds, make 4 rnds Orange and 4 rnds Green. Break off and fasten. Attach Blue.

BRIM: Rnd 1: With Blue, rep 4th rnd of Crown—66 sc. **Rnd 2:** Ch 1, sc in same sc as joining, sc in each sc. Join. **Rnds 3–4:** Rep last 2 rnds—72 sc. Break off Blue. Attach Amethyst. **Next 4 Rnds:** With Amethyst, rep last 4 rnds—84 sc. Break off Amethyst; attach Black. With Black, work 2 rnds even. **Last Rnd:** Work from **left to right,** * insert hook in next sc to the **right** and complete a sc; rep from * around. Join with sl st to first sc. Break off and fasten. Double elastic and draw through last rnd of Crown, adjust to fit and sew ends together securely.

GARTER-STITCH CAPE

SIZE: Excluding fringe, 38″ down center back; 6 yds wide across lower edge.

MATERIALS: Bucilla Knitting Worsted, 4 Ply or Fleisher's Twin-Pak Superior Worsted, 4 Ply (4 oz paks): 9 paks. Circular Needle, Size 10½–29″ length OR SIZE TO OBTAIN GAUGE. Crochet Hook, Size H.

GAUGE: Garter st, 10 sts = 3″; 12 rows (6 ridges) = 2″

TO MAKE: Cast on 54 sts—neck edge.
Note: Work is done in rows; do not join. Turn.
Row 1 (right side): K 3, yo, k 11, * place a marker on needle, yo, k 13; rep from * once, place a marker on needle, yo, k rem 14 sts —58 sts. **Row 2:** K 3, yo, * k to marker, sl marker, yo; rep from * twice, k to end—62 sts. Rep Row 2 until there are 578 sts. Bind off loosely as to k. Do not break off. Slip rem st onto crochet hook.

BORDER: Row 1: With attached yarn and crochet hook, ch 5, turn, skip first st, sc in next st, * ch 5, skip 2 sts, sc in next st; rep from * along entire bound-off edge—193 lps. **Row 2:** Ch 6, turn, sc in first lp, * ch 6, sc in next lp; rep from * across. **Row 3:** Same as Row 2. **Rows 4 and 5:** Same as Row 2, but working ch 7 instead of ch 6 for each lp. **Rows 6 and 7:** Same as Row 2, but working ch 8 instead of ch 6. **Rows 8 and 9:** Same as Row 2, but working ch 9 instead of ch 6. Break off and fasten.

Fringe: Wind yarn several times around an 8″ piece of cardboard; cut at one end. Continue to cut strands as needed. Hold 4 strands tog and fold in half to form a loop. With crochet hook draw loop of strands through a crocheted lp on last row, slip loose ends through lp on hook and pull tightly. Tie 4 strands in same way in each lp along last row. Trim fringe evenly. Steam lightly.

51

MIMIC TOP

SIZES: Directions are for small size (6–8). Changes for medium (10–12) and large (14–16) sizes are in parentheses. Top fits snugly.

NOTE: You can duplicate any multi-color striped fabric, using as many colors as desired. Except for the first and last stripe, vary width of all other stripes from 1 to 5 rnds as you wish (see photo), making your own arrangement of colors. Change colors at end of rnd. Break off and fasten strands not in use.

MATERIALS: Brunswick Germantown Knitting Worsted, 4 Ply or Windrush, 4 Ply (4 oz skn): 1 skn #414 Purple for main color; parts of skns or scraps of as many colors as desired. Circular Needles, Nos. 5 and 8–24"

length OR SIZE TO OBTAIN GAUGE.

GAUGE: Stockinette st, 5 sts = 1"; 6 rnds = 1".

BLOCKING MEASUREMENTS: Bust (stretched) 30 (33–37)".

TO MAKE: Start at lower edge with Purple and No. 5 needle, cast on 130 (140–150) sts. Join, being careful not to twist sts—this is center back. Work in garter st (k 1 rnd, p 1 rnd) for 1", inc 10 sts evenly spaced around on last rnd—140 (150–160) sts. Change to No. 8 needle and to next color. Making stripes as directed, work in rnds of stockinette st (k each rnd) until length is 10 (10–10½)" from beg or to within one inch of desired length. Change back to No. 5 needle

and with a different color or main color if desired, work in garter st for 1" for top border. Bind off.

Strap (Make 2): With No. 5 needle and same color used for last stripe, cast on 6 sts. Work back and forth in rows of garter st (k each row) until strap measures about 10" or desired length. Bind off.

FINISHING: Block to measurement. Place tube flat on a flat surface with end of rnds at center back. With pins mark center front and center back on top edge, then mark position of straps, having markers about 3 (3½–3¾)" at each side of center front marker and 2¾ (3–3¼)" at each side of center back marker. With ends of straps on wrong side of top border, sew straps in place.

BRAID-TRIMMED VEST AND HEAD SCARF

SIZES: Directions are for size 8–10. Changes for size 12–14 are in parentheses.

MATERIALS: Bucilla Wool and Shetland Wool (1¾ oz) balls. **VEST:** 4 (5). **HEAD SCARF:** 1. Knitting needles, No. 8 OR SIZE TO OBTAIN GAUGE. Crochet hook Size F.

GAUGE: 5 sts = 1″, 7 rows = 1″.

BACK: Cast on 87(95) sts. + Work in Garter st (K every row) for 9 rows. **Rib Pattern: Row 10(right side):**P1, * K1, P1, rep from * across. **Row 11:**P. Rep Rows 10 and 11, 3 times more, then rep Row 10 once more. + These 18 rows form pat. Rep between +'s 3 times more, ending ready for a right side row.

SHAPE ARMHOLES: Keeping to pats bind off 7(8) sts at beg of next 2 rows. Dec 1 st each end every other row 7 times. 59(65) sts. Work until armholes measure 8″ from beg, ending ready for a right side row.

SHAPE SHOULDERS: Bind off 6(7) sts at beg of next 4 rows, then bind off 7(8) sts at beg of next 2 rows. Bind off remaining 21 sts for back of neck.

LEFT FRONT: Cast on 43(47) sts. Work at back until piece measures same length to underarm, ending at side edge.

SHAPE ARMHOLES AND NECK: Bind off 7(8) sts at side edge, work to last 2sts, K2 tog. Dec 1 st at armhole edge every other row 7 times and at neck edge every 6th row 9 times more. 19(22) sts. Work until armhole measures same as back to shoulder, ending at side edge.

SHAPE SHOULDER: Bind off 6(7) sts every other row 2 times, then bind off remaining 7(8) sts.

RIGHT FRONT: Work same as left front reversing shaping.

FINISHING: Sew shoulder and side seams.

BRAID: Lower Edging: Cut 21 strands of yarn 90″ long. Fold in half and tie tightly at fold. Divide 42 strands into 3 parts of 14 strands. Make a braid. Sew braid evenly around lower edge. Cut off excess. **Neck Edging and Tassels:** Cut 21 strands of yarn 70″ long. Fold in half. Tie tightly about 6½″ below folded edge forming a tassel, cut folded edge. Make a braid long enough to fit smoothly from beg of neck shaping to end of neck shaping on other side. Fasten tightly leaving end for other tassel. To complete tassel wind 2 strands of yarn 10 times around tassel about 1″ below tied end. Trim to desired length. Sew to neck edge leaving tassels free. **Front Edging (make 2):** Cut 21 strands 30″ long. Fold in half and tie tightly. Make a braid to fit front edge from beg of neck shaping to lower edge. Fasten tightly, leaving end for tassel. Make a tassel as be-fore. Sew to fronts, having top of braid under neck tassel and front tassel over lower edging. Tack down knotted sections of tassels.

ARMHOLES (make 2): Cut 21 strands 63″ long. Work a braid as on lower edging until long enough to fit around armhole. Sew to armhole edge. **BLOCK.**

HEAD SCARF: Cast on 3 sts. **Row 1:** Inc 1 st in first st, K1, inc 1 st in last st. 5 sts. **Row 2:** K. **Row 3:** Inc 1 st in first st, K to last st, inc 1 st in last st. 7 sts. **Row 4:** K. Rep Rows 3 and 4 until there are 97 sts on needle. Bind off.

TIES (make 2): With F hook ch 41. Sl st in 2nd ch from hook and each ch to end. Fasten off. Sew 1 tie to each end of bound off edge.

BRAID: Cut 12 strands of yarn 130″ long. Fold in half and tie tightly at fold. Divide 24 strands into 3 parts of 8 strands. Make a braid long enough to go around 3 sides of scarf. Sew braid to scarf, beg and ending at back point of scarf.

TASSEL: Cut 21 strands 12″ long. Fold in half and tie tightly at fold. Wind 2 strands of yarn 10 times around tassel about 1″ below tied end. Trim ends. Sew to back point of scarf covering braid joining.

SIZE: Directions are for medium size.

MATERIALS: Bernat Sesame "4" (4 oz balls): 18 balls Charcoal Heather (0); 3 Oyster White (W), 2 each Scarlet (R), Geranium (B) and Mahogany (Br). Knitting Needles, 1 pair No. 5 OR SIZE TO OBTAIN GAUGE. 7" zipper, Grosgrain ribbon, 7 buttons.

GAUGE: Stockinette st, 6 sts = 1"; 8 rows = 1".

BLOCKING MEASUREMENTS: Coat—Width of back at underarm—18". Width of each front at underarm—12". Width of sleeve at upper arm—13½".

COAT

BACK: Using O, cast on 168 sts. Work in garter st (k each row) for lower border as follows: With O work 14 rows; with B work 8 rows; with W work 12 rows, with Br work 8 rows—42 rows. Continuing to work in garter st, with O work 12 rows, with R work 14 rows, then repeat first 42 rows once—110 rows in all. With O only, work in stockinette st (k 1 row, p 1 row) until length is 11¾" from beg, end with a p row. **Next Row:** K 15, place a marker on needle; k 2 tog, k 45, sl 1, k 1, psso, place a marker on needle; k 40, place a marker on needle; sl 1, k 1, psso, k 45, k 2 tog, place a marker on needle; k 15—4 sts decreased. Slipping markers on every row and continuing in stockinette st, work even for 1½", end with a p row. Dec as before one st after first and 3rd markers and one st before 2nd and 4th markers (4 sts in all) on next k row and every 1½" thereafter 14 times in all—108 sts rem. Work even until total length is 39½" from beg. Inc one st at each end of next row—110 sts. Work even until length is 44" from beg.

ARMHOLES: Bind off 6 sts at beg of next 2 rows. Bind off 3 sts at beg of following 2 rows. Bind off 2 sts at beg of next 4 rows. Dec one st each end every other row twice —80 sts. Work even until armholes measure 7".

SHOULDERS: Bind off 7 sts at beg of next 4 rows, 8 sts at beg of following 2 rows. Bind off rem 36 sts.

LEFT FRONT: With O, cast on 88 sts. Work lower border as for Back—110 rows. Break off. Place sts on a st holder. **Front Band:** With O, cast on 16 sts and work in stockinette st until piece measures same as lower border of Front, end with a k row. Half of the

16 sts will be folded to wrong side for facing. **Next Row:** With wrong side facing, p across; place the 88 Front sts on free needle and p across these sts—104 sts. With O only and starting with a k row, work in stockinette st until total length is 11¾" from beg, end with a p row. **Next Row:** K 15, place a marker on needle; k 2 tog, k 54, k 2 tog, place a marker on needle; k 31—2 decs made. Continuing in stockinette st throughout and slipping markers on every row, dec one st after first marker and one st before 2nd marker on a k row every 1½" 10 more times, then every 1½" 6 times—70 sts. Work even until length is 38" from beg. Inc one st at side edge on next row and again after 4"–72 sts. Work even until length is 44" from beg, end at side edge.

ARMHOLE: At side edge bind off 6 sts once, then at same edge bind off 3 sts once, 2 sts every other row twice. Dec st at same edge every other row twice—57 sts. Work even until armhole measures 4½", end at front edge.

NECK: At front edge bind off 15 sts at beg of next row. At same edge bind off 3 sts every other row twice, 2 sts every other row 5 times. Dec one st at same edge on every row 4 times—22 sts rem. If necessary, work even until armhole measures 7", end at armhole edge.

SHOULDER: At armhole edge, bind off 7 sts every other row twice, 8 sts once. With pins mark the position of 6 buttons evenly spaced along front band, with first pin 25" up from lower edge and last pin 3½" below neck edge. Buttonholes will be made on Right Front to correspond with pins. **To make a buttonhole:** Starting at front edge, work one st, bind off next 4 sts (for buttonhole on facing); work next 7 sts, bind off next 4 sts; complete row. On next row, cast on 4 sts over each set of bound-off sts.

RIGHT FRONT: Making buttonholes in line with pins on Left Front, work to correspond with Left Front, reversing all shaping.

SLEEVES: Using O, cast on 60 sts. Work 6 rows in garter st. Continuing in garter st, work 14 rows R; 14 rows O; 8 rows B; 12 rows W; 8 rows Br, then with O only, work in stockinette st, increasing one st each end every inch 11 times—82 sts. Work even until length is 17½" from beg.

Top Shaping: Bind off 6 sts at beg of next 2 rows, bind off 2 sts at beg of each of next 6 rows. Dec one st each end every other row 16 times. Bind off 2 sts at beg of next 6 rows.

Bind off rem 14 sts.

POCKET (Make 2): With O, cast on 42 sts. Work in stockinette st for 5½". Work in k 1, p 1 ribbing for 1¼". Bind off in ribbing.

HOOD: Back Panel: With O, cast on 41 sts. Work in stockinette st for 11¾", end with a p row. Break off yarn. Leave sts on needle. With O and right side facing, pick up and k 70 sts along side edge of panel, then k across the 41 sts of panel, pick up and k 70 along other side edge—181 sts. Work in garter st for 9 rows. Continuing in garter st, work 8 rows B; 12 rows W; 8 rows Br; 12 rows O; 14 rows R; 16 rows O. Bind off.

FINISHING: Steam pieces lightly to measurements; do not press. Sew side, shoulder and sleeve seams. Sew in sleeves. Sew lower section of front bands to front edges. Fold front bands in half lengthwise, to wrong side, matching buttonholes and stitch in place. Buttonhole st around buttonholes.

Neckband: With O and right side facing, starting at right front corner of neck, pick up and k 4 sts, skip next 4 sts, cast on 4 sts for buttonhole, pick up and k evenly 112 sts along entire neck edge. Work in k 1, p 1 ribbing for ¾". Bind off in ribbing. Sew hood to neck edge, with back panel along back of neck and easing in front sections to fit. Sew pockets in place, sew on buttons.

SKIRT

BACK PANEL: With O, cast on 104 sts. Work border as follows: Working in garter st, work 6 rows O; 14 rows R; 14 rows O; 8 rows B; 12 rows O; 8 rows Br. With O, work in stockinette st until length is 7" from beg. Dec one st each end on next row and every inch thereafter 20 more times, then dec one st each end every ¾" 8 times—46 sts. Work even until length is 35½" from beg. Bind off.

FRONT PANEL: Work same as Back Panel.

SIDE PANEL (Make 2): With O, cast on 85 sts. Work as for Back Panel until length is 27". Continuing decs at side edges as for Back Panel **at the same time,** dec one st at center of row for dart on next row and every 2¼" thereafter 3 times in all. Work even until length is 35½" from beg. Bind off rem 24 sts.

FINISHING: Sew the 4 panels tog, leaving 7" free at front left seam for zipper opening. Sew in zipper. Sew ribbon inside waist, adjusting to desired size. Steam lightly.

PLAID DRESS

SIZES: Directions are for size 8. Changes for sizes 10, 12 and 14 are in parentheses.

MATERIALS: Spinnerin Sport (2-oz ball): 12 (12–13–14) balls A, Blue Heather, and 3 (3–4–4) balls each B, Navy and C, White. Knitting Needles, No. 6 OR SIZE TO OBTAIN GAUGE. Circular Needle, No. 6 (29″ length). Crochet Hook, Size G. Zippers, 4″ neck and 7″ dress. Round elastic.

GAUGE: 11 sts = 2″; 8 rows = 1″.

BLOCKING MEASUREMENTS: Bust—32 (34–36–38)″. Width of back or front at underarm—16 (17–18–19)″. Width of sleeve at upper arm—15 (15–16–16)″. Width of skirt at lower edge—58 (60–62–64)″.

NOTE: The horizontal stripes are knitted in the pattern. The vertical stripes are crocheted over the p sts after pcs have been completed.

SKIRT-BACK: With straight needles and A, cast on 161 (167–173–177) sts. **Row 1 (right side):** With A, k 2 (5–8–10), p 1, * k 9, p 1, (k 2, p 1) twice; k 9, p 1; rep from * across, end with k 2 (5–8–10). **Row 2:** P 2 (5–8–10), k 1, * p 9, k 1, (p 2, k 1) twice; p 9, k 1; rep from * across, end with p 2 (5–8–10). **Rows 3–12:** Rep Rows 1 and 2. Drop A. **Rows 13–14:** With B, rep Rows 1 and 2. Break off B. **Rows 15–16:** With A, rep Rows 1 and 2. Drop A. **Rows 17–22:** Working as for Rows 1 and 2, work 2 rows C, 2 rows A and 2 rows B. Break off C and B. **Rows 23–34:** With A, rep Rows 1 and 2. Drop A. **Rows 35–36:** With C, work 2 rows as before. Break off C. These 36 rows form pat. Keeping continuity of pat, dec one st ea end of next row and every 2″ thereafter 6 more times; every 1½″ 6 times; every 1″ 5 times —125 (131–137–141) sts. Keeping in pat, work even until length is 32″ from beg or desired length to waistline (allowing 5 additional inches for ruffle). Bind off.

FRONT: Work same as Back of Skirt.

RUFFLE: Start at inner edge of hem with circular needle and A, cast on 655 (661–667–671) sts. Do not join. Work in rows. Starting with Row 23, work in pat as for Back of Skirt for 48 rows. **Next Row:** With A, * k 2 tog; rep from * across, end with k 1. P 1 row. Bind off.

BODICE-BACK: With straight needles and A, cast on 77 (81–87–93) sts. **Row 1:** K 0 (1–4–7), p 0 (1–1–1), * k 9, p 1, (k 2, p 1) twice; k 9, p 1; rep from * across, ending last rep with p 0 (1–1–1), k 0 (1–4–7). **Row 2:** P 0 (1–4–7), k 0 (1–1–1), * p 9, k 1, (p 2, k 1) twice; p 9, k 1; rep from * across, ending last rep with k 0 (1–1–1), p 0 (1–4–7). Keeping in pat as established and starting with Row 3, work as for Back of Skirt, increasing one st ea end every 6th row 6 (7–7–7) times in all, working inc sts in pat—89 (95–101–107) sts. Work even until length is 7 (7–7½–7¾)″ from beg.

ARMHOLES: Keeping continuity of pat, bind off 6 (6–7–7) sts at beg of next 2 rows. Dec one st ea end every other row 2 (3–4–5) times—73 (77–79–83) sts. Work even until armholes length is 2½ (2½–3–3)″, end with wrong-side row.

BACK OPENING: Work in pat over 37 (39–40–42) sts; attach another ball of yarn, with this strand cast on one st on right-hand needle and work across rem 36 (38–39–41) sts. Work even ea side with separate yarn until armholes measure 6½ (6¾–7–7½)″.

SHOULDERS: From armhole edge of ea side bind off 8 sts once; 7 (8–8–9) sts twice. From same edge, bind off rem 15 (15–16–16) sts for back of neck.

FRONT: Work same as Back of Bodice to within back opening. Continue to work even until length of armhole is 4 (4–4½–4½)″.

NECK: Work in pat over 26 (28–29–31) sts; attach another ball of yarn and with this strand bind off 21 sts for center front of neck; complete row. Work ea side with separate yarn; dec one st at neck edge every other row 4 (4–5–5) times. Work even over 22 (24–24–25) sts until armholes are same as back.

SHOULDERS: From armhole edge of ea side, bind off 8 sts once; 7 (8–8–9) sts twice.

SLEEVES: With straight needles and A, cast on 81 (81–87–87) sts. K 1 row; p 1 row for hem. P next row for hemline. Work in pat as for Back of Bodice Size 10 (10–12–12) for about 3″ from hemline, ending with same pat row as on back before armholes.

TOP SHAPING: Keeping continuity of pat, bind off 6 (6–7–7) sts at beg of next 2 rows. Dec one st ea end every 6th row 6 (6–7–7) times. Work 0 (2–0–4) rows even. Bind off.

VERTICAL STRIPES: In ea section of "p 1, k 2, p 1, k 2 and p 1", use C for center stripe, use B for stripes at ea side of center C stripe. For all single stripes between "k 9" sections use C. Starting at lower edge, hold yarn on wrong side and with crochet hook on right side, work sl st over ea row of p st line from lower edge to top edge, being careful not to pull in work. Break off and fasten. Work vertical stripes in this manner throughout ea piece, using colors as designated.

FINISHING: Steam pieces lightly through a damp cloth to measurements; do not press. Sew skirt side seams, leaving 4″ open at top of left seam. Sew ends of ruffle tog. Using a large needle, run a long strand along top edge of ruffle, gather to fit lower edge of skirt and with seam at right seam of skirt sew ruffle in place. Turn 1″ hem along lower edge of ruffle and stitch in place. With A, crochet 1 row of sl st over joining of ruffle to skirt. Sew side seams of bodice, leaving a 3″ opening at lower end of left seam. Sew shoulder and sleeve seams. Sew in sleeves gathering top to fit. Cut elastic to desired length for gathering lower edge of ea sleeve, allowing ½″ for sewing; sew ends of ea piece tog securely. Turn sleeve hems to wrong side over elastic and stitch in place. Gather top of skirt to fit lower edge of bodice, with left side openings matching, sew skirt to bodice. With A, from right side, sc evenly along neck edge and back opening, being careful to keep work flat. Join with sl st to first sc. Break off and fasten. Sc evenly along edges of side opening. Join. Break off and fasten. Sew in zippers.

SIZES: Directions are for Size 38. Changes for Sizes 40, 42 and 44 are in parentheses.

MATERIALS: Craft Yarns "Norska", 3½ oz. skein—9 (10, 11, 12) skeins. No. 8 knitting needles, OR SIZE TO OBTAIN GAUGE. Size G aluminum crochet hook. 10 buttons.

GAUGE: 4 sts = 1".

BACK: Cast on 76 (80, 84, 88) sts. **Row 1:** Wrong side. K 5, p 66 (70, 74, 78), k 5. **Row 2:** K. Repeat Rows 1 and 2 for 13 times. **Next Row:** P across, increasing 1 st each end—78 (82, 86, 90) sts. Change to stock. st and work even until 18" from beg, or desired length to underarm, ending with a p row.

SHAPE ARMHOLES: Bind off 5 sts beg next 2 rows. Dec 1 st each end every other row 4 times—60 (64, 68, 72) sts. Work even until armholes measure 8½ (9, 9½, 10)".

SHAPE SHOULDERS: Row 1: Bind off 6 (7, 8, 9) sts, work across next 16 sts, turn. **Row 2:** Dec 1 st at beg of next row (neck edge), complete row. **Row 3:** Bind off 7 sts, complete row. **Row 4:** Dec 1 st at neck edge, complete row. Bind off remaining 7 sts. Attach yarn and bind off center 16 (18, 20, 22) sts for neck, work across remaining 22 (23, 24, 25) sts. Work to correspond to other side, reversing shaping.

RIGHT FRONT: Cast on 42 (44, 46, 48) sts. **Row 1:** Wrong side. K 5, p 31 (33, 35, 37), k 6 (front border). **Row 2:** K. Repeat Rows 1 and 2 for 13 times. **Next row:** Inc 1 st at beg of row, p across to within last 6 sts, k 6 (front border). Change to stock. st, keeping 6 sts garter st (k every row) at front edge. Work to underarm as for back.

SHAPE ARMHOLE: At arm edge, bind off 5

sts once, dec 1 st every other row 4 times—34 (36, 38, 40) sts. Work even until armhole measures 5½ (6, 6½, 7)", ending at front edge.

SHAPE NECK: Bind off 9 (10, 11, 12) sts, complete row. At neck edge, bind off 2 sts once, then dec 1 st every other row 3 times—20 (21, 22, 23) sts. Work to shoulder as for back.

SHAPE SHOULDER: At arm edge, bind off 6 (7, 8, 9) sts once, 7 sts every other row twice. Mark for 6 buttons evenly spaced, placing first 3" from lower edge and last ½" below neck shaping.

LEFT FRONT: Work to correspond to Right Front, reversing shaping and working in buttonholes opposite markers for buttons.

BUTTONHOLE: Work to within 4 sts from front edge, bind off 2 sts, complete row. **Next row:** Cast on 2 sts above bound off sts of previous row.

RIGHT SLEEVE: Cast on 36 (38, 40, 42) sts. Work 10 rows garter st. **Next row:** K to within last 4 sts, bind off next 2 sts, k to end. **Next row:** K 2, cast on 2 sts above bound off sts, k to end. Work 10 rows garter st. **Next row:** K first 13 (14, 15, 16) sts, cast on 1 st, turn. **Next row:** P 14 (15, 16, 17) sts. Work on these 14 (15, 16, 17) sts in stock. st for 6 more rows. Break yarn and hold on a holder. Cast on 1 st, working across remaining 23 (24, 25, 26) sts—24 (25, 26, 27) sts. Work on these sts in stock. st until there are 8 sts in all (same number of rows as other side). **Next row:** Work 24 (25, 26, 27) sts, then onto same needle work the 14 (15, 16, 17) sts from first section—38 (40, 42, 44) sts. Work in stock. st and inc 1 st each end of

next row, then every 1¼" for 9 times more—58 (60, 62, 64) sts. Work even until 19" from beg, or desired length to underarm.

SHAPE CAP: Bind off 5 sts beg next 2 rows. Dec 1 st each end every other row 11 (12, 13, 14) times, then every row 4 times. Bind off 2 sts beg next 2 rows. Bind off.

LEFT SLEEVE: Work same as for Right Sleeve for 10 rows. **Next row:** K 2, bind off 2, k to end. **Next row:** K and cast on 2 sts above bound off sts. Work 10 rows garter st. **Next row:** K 23 (24, 25, 26) sts, cast on 1 st—24 (25, 26, 27) sts, turn. Work stock. st on these 24 (25, 26, 27) sts for 7 rows more. Break yarn. Cast on 1 st, work across 13 (14, 15, 16) sts—14 (15, 16, 17) sts. Work on these sts for 8 rows (same number of rows as for first section). Join and work to correspond to Right Sleeve.

COLLAR: Cast on 24 (26, 28, 30) sts. Work garter st, casting on 8 sts at end of next 6 rows—72 (74, 76, 78) sts. Work even in garter st until 4" from last cast-on row. Bind off loosely.

POCKET: Make 2. Cast on 18 (18, 20, 20) sts. Work stock. st for 4½". Work 4 rows garter st. **Next row:** K 8 (8, 9, 9) sts, bind off 2 sts, k 8 (8, 9, 9) sts. **Next row:** K across, cast on 2 sts above bound off sts. Work 3 rows garter st. Bind off.

FINISHING: Sew shoulders and sleeve seams. Sew side seams, starting from vent opening. Sew in sleeves. Sew on collar to within ¾" of front edges. Sew on pockets as shown. Crochet 1 row of sc along side openings of sleeves. With right side facing, crochet 1 row of sc across lower edge, making sure work lies flat. Steam lightly on wrong side. Sew on buttons.

BOY'S STRIPED SWEATER

SIZES: Directions are for Size 8. Changes for Sizes 10 and 12 are in parentheses.

MATERIALS: Craft Yarns "Krona", 1.8 oz. skein. 4 (5, 6) Blue (A), 3 (4, 5) Off White (B). Nos. 4 and 5 knitting needles, OR SIZE TO OBTAIN GAUGE No. 4 (16") circular knitting needle. 3 small buttons.

GAUGE: 5 sts = 1".

STRIPE PATTERN: Work in stock. st in the following color sequence: 6 rows A, 2 B, 2 A, 2 B, 6 A, 6 B, 2 A, 2 B, 2 A, 6 B. These 36 rows form stripe pattern.

BACK: With No. 4 needles and A, cast on 68 (72, 78) sts. Work stock. st for 5 rows (hem). K 1 row on wrong side (hemline). Change to No. 5 needles and work as follows: **Row 1:** (K 1, p 1) twice, k 60 (64, 70), (p 1, k1) twice. **Row 2:** (P 1, k1) twice, p 60 (64, 70), (k 1, p 1) twice. Repeat Rows 1 and 2 twice. **Row 7:** Rib 4 A as established, attach B, k 60 (64, 70) B, attach another ball A, rib 4 A as established. **Note:** When changing colors always twist yarns on wrong side to prevent holes. **Row 8:** Rib 4 A, p 60 (64, 70) B, rib 4 A. **Rows 9 and 10:** Repeat Rows 1 and 2. **Rows 11 and 12:** Repeat Rows 7 and 8. **Rows 13 through 18:** Repeat Rows 1 and 2. **Row 19:** With B, cast on 1 st, k across row, increasing 1 st in last st—70 (74, 80) sts. **Row 20:** With B, p across. Continue in stripe pattern until 12 (13, 14)" from hemline, or desired length to armhole.

SHAPE ARMHOLES: Bind off 5 sts beg next 2 rows. Dec 1 st each end every other row 3 (3, 4) times—54 (58, 62) sts. Work even until armhole measures 5½ (6, 6½)".

SHAPE SHOULDERS: Bind off 8 sts, work next 9 (10, 11) sts, turn. Dec 1 st at beg of next row, complete row. Bind off remaining 8 (9, 10) sts. Place center 20 (22, 24) sts on a holder for back of neck, attach yarn and work other side to correspond, reversing shaping.

FRONT: Work same as for back to underarm, ending with a p row.

SHAPE ARMHOLE: Left Front: Bind off 5 sts at arm edge, k 27 (29, 32) sts, turn. Continue in pattern and dec 1 st at arm edge every other row 3 (3, 4) times—24 (26, 28) sts. Work even until armhole measures 3½ (4, 4½)", ending at neck edge.

SHAPE NECK: Work 5 (6, 7) sts and place on a holder, complete row. Dec 1 st at neck edge every other row 3 times—16 (17, 18) sts. Work even to shoulder as back.

SHAPE SHOULDER: At arm edge, bind off 8 once, 8 (9, 10) sts. Attach yarn at neck opening, bind off center 6 sts. Work Right Front to correspond to Left Front, reversing shaping.

SLEEVES: Note: Determine length of sleeve needed. We used approx. 12 (13, 14)" to underarm. Measure stripe pattern from top of back down to determine at what point of pattern you start at in order to end at armhole with same pattern row as at underarm of back. With No. 4 needles and A, cast on 38 (40, 42) sts. Work hem and hemline as for back. Change to No. 5 needles and stripe pattern. Inc 1 st each end of next row, then every 1¼" 8 (8, 9) times more—56 (58, 62)

sts. Work even until 12 (13, 14)" from hemline, or desired length, ending with same pattern row as at underarm of back.

SHAPE CAP: Bind off 5 sts beg next 2 rows. Dec 1 st each end every other row 8 (9, 10) times, every row 4 times. Bind off 2 sts beg next 4 rows. Bind off.

FRONT AND NECK BORDERS: Sew shoulder seams. With circular needle, A and right side facing, starting at right front edge, pick up 26 (28, 30) sts to neck shaping, place a marker, pick up 43 (45, 47) sts around entire neck to other neck shaping, place a marker, pick up 26 (28, 30) sts along other front edge. Turn. **Row 1:** * K 1, p 1; repeat from * to 1 st before marker, inc 1 st in next st, slip marker, inc 1 st in next st, work ribbing to 1 st before next marker, inc 1 st in next st, slip marker, inc 1 st in next st, complete row. **Row 2:** Work ribbing as established, slipping markers. **Row 3:** Repeat Row 1. **Row 4:** Right side facing. **Buttonhole Row:** Rib to within 28 (30, 32) sts from end, rib 1, (yo, p 2 tog, rib 10) twice, yo, p 2 tog, complete row. **Row 5:** Repeat Row 1, working a st over each yo. **Row 6:** As Row 2. **Row 7:** As Row 1. Bind off in ribbing.

FINISHING: Sew side seams, leaving first 18 rows from hemline open for side vents. Sew sleeve seams. Sew in sleeves. Turn all hems to wrong side and sew in place. Overlap base of left side of neck border over right side and sew to 6 st bind-off. Sew on buttons. **DO NOT BLOCK OR PRESS.** Wet block (Wet garment with cold water. Lay on a towel to measurements. Dry away from heat and sun).

CHILD'S FAIR ISLE SWEATER

SIZES: Directions are for Size 6. Changes for Sizes 8 and 10 are in parentheses.

MATERIALS: Unger's Britania, 1⁹⁄₁₀ oz. ball.

SWEATER: 2 (2, 3) Blue (A), 1 (2, 2) Purple (B) and 1 each of Grey (C), Pink (D). HAT: 1 each of A, B, C and D.

Knitting needles Nos. 4 and 6 OR SIZE TO OBTAIN GAUGE. 1 tapestry needle.

GAUGE: 11 sts = 2″; 13 rows = 2″.

NOTE: Carry yarn loosely across back of work to prevent drawing in. Animal figures are embroidered in duplicate st (p. 13) when pieces are completed.

SWEATER BACK: With No. 4 needles and A, cast on 71 (77, 83) sts. Work in k 1, p 1 ribbing for 1 (1½, 2)″. Change to No. 6 needles and Stock. St. Work rows 1 through 4 of Chart 1, following sizes as indicated. Work 20 rows C (Note: Animal figures will be worked in duplicate st on this C band when pieces are completed). Work 17 rows Chart 2, 3 rows A, 6 rows Chart 1, 4 rows A, work 0 (2, 4) rows Chart 3.

SHAPE ARMHOLES: Working Chart 3, bind off 4 (5, 5) sts beg next 2 rows, dec 1 st each end every other row 4 (4, 5) times—55 (59, 63) sts. Work 2 rows C, 17 rows Chart 2, 3 rows A. Complete remainder of armhole with as many rows as is needed of 6 rows Chart 1, 4 rows A.

When armholes measure 5 (5½, 6)″, **SHAPE SHOULDERS:** Bind off 4 (5, 6) sts beg next 2 rows, then 5 sts beg next 4 rows —27 (29, 31) sts.

BACK NECKBAND: Change to No. 4 needles and A. Work in k 1, p 1 ribbing for 1¾″ Bind off in ribbing.

FRONT: Work same as back until armholes measure 3 (3½, 4)″—55 (59, 63) sts.

SHAPE NECK: Continue in patterns as back. Work 19 (20, 21) sts. Slip remaining sts to a holder. At neck edge, dec 1 st every row 2 times, every other row 3 times—14 (15, 16) sts. Work to shoulder as for back.

SHAPE SHOULDER: At arm edge, bind off 4 (5, 6) sts once, 5 sts every other row 2 times. Leave center 17 (19, 21) sts on holder, slip remaining 19 (20, 21) sts onto needle. Attach yarn at neck edge and work to correspond to other side, reversing shaping.

SLEEVES: With No. 4 needles and A, cast on 35 (39, 43) sts. Work in k 1, p 1 ribbing for 1½ (2, 2½)″. Change to No. 6 needles and Stock St. Inc 1 st each end every 8th row 8 times, working in pattern as follows: Work 0 (0, 2) row A, 6 rows Chart 1, 2 (4, 4) rows A, 16 rows Chart 3, 0 (2, 4) rows C, 17 rows Chart 2, 3 rows A, 6 rows Chart 1, 4 rows A, 0 (2, 4) rows Chart 3.

SHAPE CAP: Continuing with Chart 3, bind off 4 (4, 5) sts beg next 2 rows. Dec 1 st each end every other row 12 (13, 14) times. When Chart 3 is completed, work 2 rows C, as many rows as needed of Chart 2, then A. Bind off 2 sts beg next 4 rows. Bind off.

FRONT NECKBAND: With No. 4 needles, A and right side facing, pick up and k 55 (57, 59) sts around front neck (this includes sts on holder). Work in k 1, p 1 ribbing as for back band. Bind off loosely in ribbing.

FINISHING: Sew shoulders and neckband seams. Mark for animal figures on C band as follows: Mark 14th (15th, 16th) st from seam edge for center of first D figure, skip 21 (23, 25) sts, mark next st for center of first A figure, skip 21 (23, 25) sts, mark next st for center of 2nd D figure. Work figures in duplicate st as marked, following Chart 5 on back and front. Sew side and sleeve seams. Sew in sleeves. Fold neckband in half to inside and sew in place. Block lightly on wrong side.

WOMAN'S FAIR ISLE SWEATER

SIZES: Directions are for Size 10. Changes for Sizes 12 and 14 are in parentheses.

MATERIALS: Unger's Britania, 1⁹⁄₁₀ oz. ball. Sweater: 3 (4, 4) Pink (A), 2 each of Purple (B), Grey (C), Blue (D).

Knitting needles Nos. 4 and 6 OR SIZE TO OBTAIN GAUGE. 1 tapestry needle.

GAUGE: 11 sts = 2″; 13 rows = 2″.

NOTE: Carry yarn loosely across back of work to prevent drawing in. Figures are embroidered in duplicate st (p. 13) when pieces are completed.

SWEATER: BACK: With No. 4 needles and A, cast on 91 (97, 103) sts. Work in k 1, p 1 ribbing for 2½″, increasing 4 sts evenly across last row—95 (101, 107) sts. Change to No. 6 needles and Stock St. Work Rows 1 through 4 of Chart 1, following sizes as indicated. Work 20 rows C (figures to be duplicate st later on this C band). Work 17 rows of Chart 2, following sizes as indicated. Work 3 rows A. Work Rows 1 through 6 of Chart 1. Work 4 rows A. Work 16 rows of Chart 3. Work 18 rows C. **SHAPE ARMHOLES:** With C, bind off 6 (6, 7) sts beg next 2 rows. Work Chart 2, **AT THE SAME TIME,** dec 1 st each end every other row 5 (6, 6) times—73 (77, 81) sts. Work 3 rows A, 6 rows Chart 1, 4 rows A, 16 rows Chart 3, 4 rows A. Start to work the 17 rows of Chart 2. **AT THE SAME TIME,** when armhole measures 7 (7¼, 7½)″, **SHAPE SHOULDERS:** Bind off 6 (7, 8) sts beg next 2 rows, 7 sts beg next 4 rows—33 (35, 37) sts. **BACK NECKBAND:** Change to No. 4 needles and work in k 1, p 1 ribbing for 2″. Bind off in ribbing.

FRONT: Work same as for back until armholes measure 4¾ (5, 5¼)″—73 (77, 81) sts. **SHAPE NECK:** Continue in pattern as back and k 26 (27, 28) sts. Slip remaining sts to a holder. At neck edge, dec 1 st every row 2 times, every other row 4 times—20 (21, 22) sts. Work even to shoulder as back. **SHAPE SHOULDER:** At arm edge, bind off 6 (7, 8) sts once, 7 sts every other row twice. Leave center 21 (23, 25) sts on holder and slip remaining 26 (27, 28) sts onto needle. Attach yarn at neck edge and work to correspond to other side, reversing shaping.

SLEEVES: With No. 4 needles and A, cast on 45 (49, 53) sts. Work in k 1, p 1 ribbing for 3″. Change to No. 6 needles and Stock St. Inc. 1 st each end every 8th row 9 times, working in patterns as follows: 6 rows of Chart 1, 4 rows A, 16 rows Chart 3, 2 rows C, 17 rows Chart 2, 3 rows A, 6 rows Chart 1, 4 rows A, 16 rows Chart 3, 2 rows C, 4 rows A, 6 rows Chart 1, 4 rows A. **SHAPE CAP:** With C, bind off 6 (6, 7) sts beg next 2 rows. Dec 1 st each end every other row 17 (18, 19) times, working 17 rows chart 2, 3 rows A, 6 rows Chart 1, 4 rows A and remainder of cap Chart 3. Bind off 2 sts beg next 4 rows. Bind off.

FRONT NECKBAND: With No. 4 needles, A and right side facing, pick up and k 61 (63, 65) sts around front of neck (this includes sts on holder). Work in k 1, p 1 ribbing as for back band. Bind off in ribbing.

FINISHING: Sew shoulder and neckband seams. Mark on C bands for figures as follows: Mark 12th (13th, 14th) st from side edge for center st of first figure (girl), * skip 17 (18, 19) sts, mark next st for center st of next figure (boy), skip 17 (18, 19) sts, mark next st for center st of next figure (girl); repeat from * once more. Follow Chart 4, working figures in duplicate st on lower and top C bands of front and back. Sew side and sleeve seams. Sew in sleeves. Fold neckband in half to inside and sew in place. Block lightly on wrong side.

continued on page 66

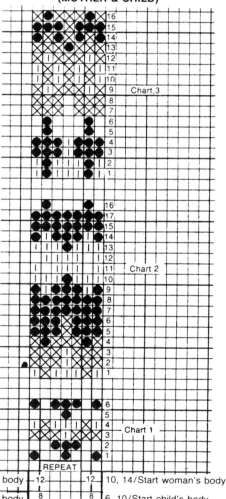

**KEY FOR FAIR ISLE SWEATERS
(MOTHER & CHILD)**

Chart 3

Chart 2

Chart 1

Key
× = **A**
○ = **B**
□ = **C**
❘ = **D**

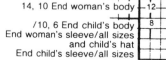

REPEAT

14, 10 End woman's body — — 10, 14/Start woman's body
/10, 6 End child's body — — 6, 10/Start child's body
End woman's sleeve/all sizes — All sizes/Start woman's
and child's hat — sleeve and child's hat
End child's sleeve/all sizes — All sizes/Start child's sleeve

SIZES: Directions are for Size 38. Changes for Sizes 40, 42 and 44 are in parentheses.

MATERIALS: Unger's Natuurwol, 1⅝ oz. ball.

SWEATER: 8 (9, 10, 11) Brown (A), 2 Natural (B) and 1 ball Unger's Britania, Rose (C). **CAP:** 2 balls A and small amounts of B and C left over from sweater. Knitting needles, Nos. 4 and 6 OR SIZE TO OBTAIN GAUGE.

GAUGE: 5 sts = 1".

NOTE: Twist yarns on wrong side when changing colors to prevent holes. Divide C into 2 equal balls.

SWEATER: BACK: With No. 4 needles and A, cast on 90 (94, 98, 102) sts. Work in k 2, p 2 ribbing for 2", increasing 6 (6, 8, 8) sts evenly across row—96 (100, 106, 110) sts. Change to No. 6 needles and Reverse Stock. St (p side is right side). Work even until 14 (14, 13½, 13½)" from beg, ending with a k row. **V BAND: Row 1:** With A, p 47 (49, 52, 54) A, attach B, k 2 B, attach 2nd ball A and p 47 (49, 52, 54) A. **Row 2:** K 46 (48, 51, 53) A, p 4 B, k 46 (48, 51, 53) A. **Row 3:** P 45 (47, 50, 52) A, k 6 B, p 45 (47, 50, 52) A. **Row 4:** K 44 (46, 49, 51) A, p 8 B, k 44 (46, 49, 51) A. **Row 5:** P 43 (45, 48, 50) A, k 10 B, p 43 (45, 48, 50) A. **Row 6:** K 42 (44, 47, 49) A, p 12 B, k 42 (44, 47, 49) A. **Row 7:** P 41 (43, 46, 48) A, k 14 B, p 41 (43, 46, 48) A. **Row 8:** K 40 (42, 45, 47) A, p 16 B, k 40 (42, 45, 47) A. **Row 9:** P 39 (41, 44, 46) A, k 8 B, attach C, k 2 C, attach 2nd ball B, k 8 B, p 39 (41, 44, 46) A. **Row 10:** K 38 (40, 43, 45) A, p 8 B, p 4 C, p 8 B, k 38 (40, 43, 45) A. **Row 11:** P 37 (39, 42, 44) A, k 8 B, k 6 C, k 8 B, p 37 (39, 42, 44) A. **Row 12:** K 36 (38, 41, 43) A, p 8 B, p 8 C, p 8 B, k 36 (38, 41, 43) A. **Row 13:** P 35 (37, 40, 42) A, k 8 B, k 4 C, k 1 B with first B ball, k 1 B with 2nd B ball, attach 2nd ball C, k 4 C, k 8 B, p 35 (37, 40, 42) A. **Row 14:** K 34 (36, 39, 41) A, p 8 B, p 4 C, p 4 B (2 sts from each B ball), p 4 C, p 8 B, k 34 (36, 39, 41) A. **Row 15:** P 33 (35, 38, 40) A, k 8 B, k 4 C, k 6 B (3 sts from each B ball), k 4 C, k 8 B, p 33 (35, 38, 40) A. **Row 16:** K 32 (34, 37, 39) A, p 8 B, p 4 C, p 8 B (4 sts from each B ball), p 4 C, p 8 B, k 32 (34, 37, 39) A. **Row 17:** P 31 (33, 36, 38) A, k 8 B, k 4 C, k 10 B (5 sts from each B ball) k 4 C, k 8 B, p 31 (33, 36, 38) A. **Row 18:** K 30 (32, 35, 37) A, p 8 B, p 4 C, p 12 B (6 sts from each B ball), p 4 C, p 8 B, k 30 (32, 35, 37) A. **Row 19:** P 29 (31, 34, 36) A, k 8 B, k 4 C, k 14 B (7 sts from each B ball), k 4 C, k 8 B, p 29 (31, 34, 36) A. **Row 20:** K 28 (30, 33, 35) A, p 8 B, p 4 C, p 16 B, p 4 C, p 8 B, k 28 (30, 33, 35) A. **Row 21:** P 27 (29, 32, 34) A, k 8 B, k 4 C, k 8 B, attach 3rd ball A, k 2 A, k 8 B, k 4 C, k 8 B, p 27 (29, 32, 34) A. **Row 22:** K 26 (28, 31, 33) A, p 8 B, p 4 C, p 8 B, With A p 1, k 2, p 1, p 8 B, p 4 C, p 8 B, k 26 (28, 31, 33) A. **Row 23:** With A p to within 1 A st before first B panel, k 8 B, k 4 C, k 8 B, with A k 1 then p to next B panel, k 1 A, k 8 B, k 4 C, k 8 B, with A p to end. **Row 24:** With A k to 1 st before first B panel, p 8 B, p 4 C, p 8 B, with A p 1 then k to next B panel, p 1 A, p 8 B, p 4 C, p 8 B, with A k to end. Continue in pattern, repeating last 2 rows 0 (2, 4, 6) times. There are 24 (24, 25, 25) A sts at each side edge.

SHAPE ARMHOLES: Keeping continuity of pattern, bind off 6 (6, 7, 7) sts beg next 2

rows. **Row 3:** K 1, sl 1, k 1, psso, work pattern to last 3 sts, k 2 tog, k 1. **Row 4:** P 2, work pattern to within last 2 sts, p 2. Repeat Rows 3 and 4 for 27 (28, 29, 30) times more—28 (30, 32, 34) sts, working in Reverse Stock. St with A only when pattern stripe is completed.

BACK NECKBAND: Change to No. 4 needles, k 1 row, increasing 2 sts evenly across for sizes 38 and 42—30 (30, 34, 34) sts. Work in k 2, p 2 ribbing for 6 rows. Bind off loosely in ribbing.

FRONT: Work same as for back until there are 62 (64, 64, 66) sts after start of armhole, ending on right side of work. **SHAPE V NECK:** Work 30 (31, 31, 32) sts in pattern, slip center 2 sts to a pin (point of V), attach another ball A, work in pattern to end. Continue armhole shaping as back, **AT THE SAME TIME,** dec 1 st at each neck edge, then every other row 11 (12, 13, 14) times more. Fasten off on last st.

SLEEVES: With No. 4 needles and A, cast on 42 (46, 50, 54) sts. Work in k 2, p 2 ribbing for 3", increasing 10 (8, 8, 6) sts evenly across last row—52 (54, 58, 60) sts. Change to No. 6 needles and Reverse Stock. St. Work 8 rows even. Inc 1 st each end of next row, then every 8th row 10 times more—74

(76, 80, 82) sts. Work even until 19" from beg, or desired length to underarm.

SHAPE CAP: Work same as for back armhole shaping. **AT THE SAME TIME,** when there are 52 (54, 56, 58) sts on needle, work stripe band as follows: Working in Stock. St. (k side used as right side), work 5 rows C, 3 rows C, 5 rows B, 1 row A. Continue in Reverse Stock. St for remainder of cap (except raglan seam sts)—6 sts. Slip remaining sts to a holder.

FINISHING: Weave sleeve caps to front.

FRONT V NECKBAND: With No. 4 needles, A and right side facing, k 6 from left sleeve holder, pick up and k 34 (36, 36, 38) sts to point of V, k 2 from pin and mark for center, pick up and k 34 (36, 36, 38) sts to right sleeve, k 6 from right sleeve holder—82 (86, 86, 90) sts. Size 38 and 44: P 2, k 2 to within 2 sts of center 2 sts, k 2 tog, p 2 center sts, k 2 tog; p 2, k 2 to end. Sizes 40 and 42: K 2, p 2 to within 2 sts of center 2 sts, k 2 tog, p 2 center sts, k 2 tog; p 2, k 2 to end. Work in ribbing as established, decreasing 1 st each side of 2 center sts for 5 rows. Bind off in ribbing. Weave sleeve caps to back armholes. Weave neckband seams. Sew side and sleeve seams. Block lightly on wrong side.

CHILD'S SWEATER   Chart 5 Duplicate st figures

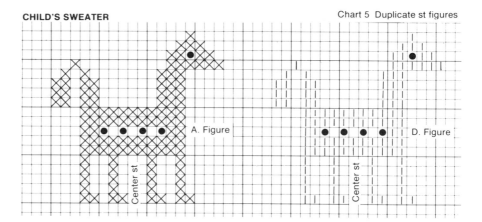

A. Figure   Center st   D. Figure   Center st

WOMAN'S SWEATER   Chart 4 Duplicate st figures

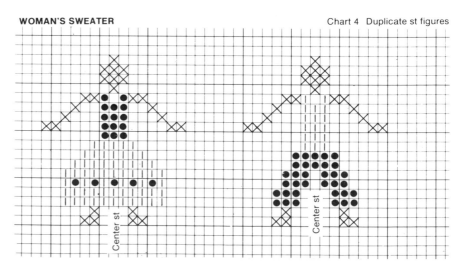

Center st   Center st

SIZES: Directions are for small (23–24″) waist. Changes for medium (25½–27″) waist and large (29″) waist are in parentheses.

NOTE: Skirt is knitted, crocheted, embroidered, braided and fringed.

MATERIALS: Coats & Clark's Red Heart "Wintuk" 4 ply (4 oz "Tangleproof" Pull-out skeins), 14 (16–17) ozs #12 Black, 12 (14–15) ozs #740 Atomic Pink, 8 (9–10) ozs #245 Orange, 3 (3–3) ozs #253 Tangerine, 1 (1–2) ozs #651 Lt Olive, 1 oz #676 Emerald for each size. Knitting Needles, No. 10½ and No. 13. One dp needle, No. 13 for cables. Crochet Hooks, sizes G, I and Q or No. 19. Skirt Zipper 7″ long. 1 yd of rose grosgrain ribbon, 1″ wide. 2 hooks & eyes. 1 yd elastic, ½″ wide. Stiff cardboard, 4″ × 7″.

GAUGE: Stockinette st on No. 10½ needles, 4 sts = 1″; 5 rows = 1″. Size I hook, 4 sc = 1″.

ACTUAL KNIT AND CROCHET MEASUREMENTS: Waistline 25 (27½–30)″. Hips 37 (40–42)″. Width across back or front at lower edge 25 (26–27)″. Length from top to lower edge with fringe 30 (31–32)″.

BACK LOWER SECTION: Beg at lower edge with Black and No. 10½ needles, cast on 100 (104–108) sts. Work in stockinette st (k 1 row, p 1 row) for 8 rows. Dec 1 st each end of next row, then every 10th row 3 times —92 (96–100) sts. Cut off Black. With Pink work in stockinette st for 9 rows. Dec 1 st each end of next row—90 (94–98) sts. Work even for 6 rows more, end right side. K 1 row on wrong side to form ridge for fringe. K 1 row. P 1 row. Bind off loosely.

FRONT LOWER SECTION: Work as for back lower section. Press both sections lightly thru a damp cloth to measure about 12″ long.

CROSSED TRIMMING: Beg at one side of back section, 1½″ up from lower edge, mark this spot with a pin. With 2nd pin mark corresponding position on opposite side edge. Divide section into 4 equal parts and mark along same row, another pin 4½″ directly above each pin of first row of pins. Cut 16 strands of Orange, each 40 (44–48)″ long. Holding these strands tog with ends extending 1″ beyond side edge, using a dble strand Orange and tapestry needle, make a couching st over these strands at first lower pinmark, * carry strands diagonally to next upper pin-mark and holding strands loosely, make a couching st as before over strands at this marker; skip the pin-mark directly below, carrying strands diagonally below, carrying strands as before; make another couching st at next lower pinmark, skip the pin-mark directly above. Rep from * across. Using another set of 16 strands, the same length as before and beg at first upper pin-mark, work in opposite direction to form crosses. Make couching sts over all strands at each crossing. Work crossed trimming on Front in same way. Sew side seams.

BOTTOM FRINGE: Wind Black yarn 30 times around 4″ cardboard. Cut lps at one edge, making 8″ strands. Cut strands as needed. Hold three 8″ strands tog and fold in half to form lp. With right side facing, insert size I hook from back to front in first st at lower edge of back section and draw lp thru; draw loose ends thru lp and tighten. Tie three 8″ strands in same way to each st around entire lower edge. Trim fringe evenly.

TOP FRINGE: Using Pink, cut strands for fringe as before. Fold three 8″ strands in half. Holding knitting with bound-off edge at top and working along the 3rd row down from top edge (ridge for fringe) insert hook upward under horizontal bar of first st on back section and draw looped end of folded strands thru, then draw loose ends thru loop and tighten. Tie three 8″ strands in same way thru horizontal bar of each st around entire top edge. Trim fringe evenly.

CROCHETED RICK RACK TRIM: With Size G hook and Olive, ch 4. **1st row:** 3 dc in 4th ch from hook. Ch 3, turn. **2nd row:** 3 dc in first dc. Ch 3, turn. Rep 2nd row until length is, without stretching, 50 (52, 54)″ or long enough to reach around entire lower edge, above the fringe. Break off and fasten. Sew rick rack trim around entire lower edge, directly above fringe.

BACK MID SECTION: Beg at side edge with Pink and No. 10½ needles, cast on 10 (12, 14) sts. **1st row:** Knit. **2nd row:** Purl, cast on 8 sts on same needle at end of row. **3rd row:** K 18 (20, 22). **4th row:** K across, cast on 8 sts at end of row—(top edge). **5th row:** K 26 (28, 30). Mark end of this row as lower edge. **6th, 7th and 8th rows:** Knit 3 rows. Now work pat as follows: **1st row** (right side): Knit. **2nd row:** Purl. **3rd through 8th row:** Knit 6 rows to form a 3-ridge panel on right side. Rep last 8 rows until total length along top edge is 18½ (20, 21)″, end last rep with knit 4 rows instead of 6. **Next row:** From top edge, bind off 8 sts, k rem sts. K 1 row. **Next row:** Bind off 8 sts, k rem sts. P 1 row. Bind off rem 10 (12, 14) sts.

FRONT MID SECTION: Work same as for Back Mid Section. Press both sections lightly through a damp cloth.

CABLE INSERTION: Holding 2 strands Tangerine tog and 2 strands Black tog, with No. 13 needles, cast on 5 Black sts, drop Black, attach Tangerine, cast on 10 Tangerine sts, drop Tangerine, pick up Black and cast on 5 Black sts. **Note:** When changing colors, always twist the unused color around the other to prevent making holes. Carry unused color loosely in back of work. **1st row:** Knit 5 Black, 10 Tangerine, 5 Black sts. **2nd row:** Using colors as established, p across. **3rd and 4th rows:** Rep first and 2nd rows. **5th row:** Place 5 Black sts onto dp needle and hold in back of work, with Tangerine k 5 Tangerine sts, with Black k the 5 sts from dp needle, place next 5 Tangerine sts onto dp needle and hold in front of work, with Black k next 5 Tangerine sts, with Tangerine k the 5 sts from dp needle. **6th row:** P 5 Tangerine, 10 Black, 5 Tangerine sts. **7th through 10th rows:** Using colors as established, work 4 rows in stockinette st. **11th row:** Place 5 sts onto dp needle and hold in back, with Black k next 5 sts, with Tangerine k the 5 sts from dp needle, place next 5 sts onto dp needle and hold in front, with Tangerine k next 5 sts, with Black, k the 5 sts from dp needle. **12th row:** P 5 Black, 10 Tangerine, 5 Black sts. Rep first through 12th rows for pat. Work in pat until strip fits, without stretching, along entire top edge of lower section of Skirt, ending with 12th row. Bind off matching colors. Sew ends tog.

Being careful to keep fringe hanging down and curving the edges of the cables on insertion, sew lower edge neatly over top edge of lower section, just above the top fringe. Sew opposite edge of insertion over lower edge of mid section, adjust edge to fit.

TOP SECTION: Beg at lower edge with Orange and Size I hook, ch 147, (157, 171) to measure, without stretching, 37 (40, 42)″. **1st row:** Sc in 2nd ch from hook and in each ch across—146 (156, 170) sc. Ch 1, turn. **2nd and 3rd rows:** Sc in each sc across. Ch 1, turn. **4th row:** Sc in first 12 (12, 14) sc, draw up a lp in each of next 2 sc, yarn over hook and draw through all 3 lps on hook—1 sc decreased; sc in each of next 22 (24, 26) sc. Rep from * 4 more times; dec 1 sc over next 2 sc, sc in rem 12 (12, 14) sc—6 sc decreased. Ch 1, turn. **5th, 6th and 7th rows:** Rep 2nd row 3 times. **8th row:** Being careful not to have decs fall directly above previous decs, sc in each sc, decreasing 6 sc evenly spaced across. Ch 1, turn. Rep last 4 rows (5th through 8th rows) until 104 (114, 122) sc remain. Break off Orange. Attach Pink, ch 1 turn. Work 3 rows even in sc for waistband. Break off and fasten. Side edges of rows form back opening. With matching colors, sc evenly along each side edge.

EMBROIDERY: Divide the 7th row into 12 equal parts and mark with pins. Working along the 19th row, with pins, mark center of each section. Making each st 6 rows high, with 2 strands of Emerald held tog and a tapestry needle, beg at first lower pin, embroider zig zag pattern in straight stitch (up to next upper pin and down to next lower pin) across top section as shown.

Having opening at center back, sew upper section to top edge of mid section. Holding 8 strands of Orange tog and using largest crochet hook, make a chain slightly larger than hip measurement. Break off and fasten all ends securely. Sew ends neatly tog. Taking sts through center back of chain, sew chain along seam between mid section and top section.

Sew zipper to back opening. Cut ribbon 3½″ longer than desired waist measurement. Form a 1½″ lp at one end of ribbon. Allowing this lp to extend beyond the left edge of back opening, easing in crochet if necessary, sew ribbon along both edges to wrong side of waistband to form casing. Cut elastic desired length and draw through casing. Sew ends securely to edges of opening. Sew hooks and eyes to ribbon. Press top section lightly through a damp cloth.

REVERSIBLE DOUBLE KNIT RUANA

SIZE: Average.

MATERIALS: Bernat Berella "4" (4 oz. balls) 50% Polyester, 50% Acrylic: 3 balls each of #8929 Geranium (A), #8922 Arbutus (B), #8967 Marine Blue (C), #8965 Navy (D), #8991 Lavender (F) and 1 skn of #8954 Orange (E). Knitting Needle, 36" circular needle Size 10 or SIZE TO OBTAIN GAUGE.

GAUGE: 4 sts = 1"; 6 rows = 1".

MEASUREMENTS: From shoulder to lower edge—28"; from arm edge to arm edge—42".

NOTE: Ruana can be knit in any combination or number of colors desired. Any number of rows of a color can be worked. There must always be the same number of rows on each side. As noted, the underside is a dark combination of colors and the top side, bright colors. We have listed the number of rows of each color on both sides as the model was made.

BRIGHT SIDE: First Half: 8 A, 4 B, 2 D, 6 F, 1 E, 4 B, 4 C, 6 A. 1 C, 1 D, 2 E, 1 D, 8 B, 3 A, 3 F, 2 A, 3 F, 3 B, 2 D, 10 A, 3 C, 8 F, 2 A, 2 B, 4 A, 4 D, 8 B, 3 C, 2 A, 2 B, 1 F, 4 E, 2 C, 6 A, 1 D. **Second Half:** 1 D, 5 B, 2 F, 2 A, 1 F, 1 E, 6 C, 3 B, 4 A, 2 D, 1 F, 2 C, 1 B, 1 F, 6 B, 2 D, 1 C, 1 A, 1 F, 2 B, 3 A, 3 C, 1 D, 2 B, 4 F, 5 E, 5 D, 2 B, 4 A, 2 C, 6 B, 1 D, 1 A, 1 B, 4 C, 6 A, 2 F, 3 B, 2 A, 2 B, 2 D, 3 C, 3 F, 5 B, 3 A, 2 E, 2 D, 2 F.

DARK SIDE: First Half: 8 D, 10 C, 8 D, 6 F, 4 D, 8 C, 12 D, 10 F, 8 D, 6 C, 10 D, 6 C, 12 D, 6 F, 6 D, 6 C. **Second Half:** 2 C, 5 D, 7 F, 10 D, 10 F, 14 D, 8 C, 7 D, 5 F, 8 D, 9 C, 10 D, 10 C, 11 D, 10 C.

Note: Cut yarn at end of every row on each side, leaving a 12" end. At the beg of each row, leave a 12" end. These ends form the fringe. Work back and forth on circular needle.

With D, loosely cast on 224 sts. **Row 1:** K in the front and back of each st across—448 sts. Cut yarn. **Double Knitting—Row 1:** With A, leaving a 12" end, * k 1, yarn in front, sl 1 as to p, yarn in back; rep from * across. **Row 2:** Turn needle around, leaving a 12" end, with D, * k 1, yarn in front, sl 1 as to p, yarn in back; rep from * across. Cut yarn leaving a 12" end. Continue as rows 1 and 2, work-

ing 1 row on dark side then one row on light side. At irregular intervals, at least every 3", work a joining row on dark side to hold knitting together. **Joining Row:** * k 1, yarn in front, sl 1, yarn in back, k 1, leave yarn in back and sl 1; rep from * across. This forms a running st on the bright side. About every 1½", pull the strands of yarn at end of rows up close to edge and knot these strands tog. Continue until piece measures approx. 21" and first half has been completed.

FRONT OPENING: K 1, k 2 tog, bind off first st, * k 2 tog, bind off; rep from * until 112 bind-offs have been made; finish row. Work next row to neck edge, cast on loosely 112 sts. **Next Row:** K in the front and back of each st on front edge, finish row. Continue until 2nd half measures same as first half. Knitting 2 sts tog, bind off all sts.

FRINGE: Tighten all knots. Divide one group of strands in half; twist each group of strands to the right for about 1½", then twist the 2 strands over each other to the left. Knot about 1½" below the first knot. Trim ends evenly.

TRI-COLOR SWEATER

SIZES: Directions for sweater are for small size 8–10. Changes for medium size 12–14 are in parentheses.

MATERIALS: Bucilla, Fleisher's or Botany Melody (1-oz ball): 8 (9) balls Bronze #12 (Color A), 3 (3) balls Turquoise #14 (Color B) and 2 (2) balls Ruby #8 (Color C). Knitting needles, 1 pair each Nos. 3, 5 and 8 OR SIZE TO OBTAIN GAUGE.

GAUGE: On No. 8 needles—9 sts = 2"; 6 rows = 1".

BLOCKING MEASUREMENTS: Bust—34 (38)". Width of back or front at underarm—17 (19)". Width of sleeve at upper arm—12 (13)".

SWEATER-BACK: Start at lower edge with A and No. 5 needles, cast on 78 (86) sts. **Ribbing: Row 1 (wrong side):** P 2, * k 2, p 2; rep from * across. **Row 2:** K 2, * p 2, k 2; rep from * across. Rep Rows 1 and 2 for 4" from beg, ending with Row 1. Change to No. 8 needles, and work in stockinette st (k 1 row, p 1 row) until total length is 10" from beg, end with a p row.

ARMHOLES: Rows 1–2: Continuing in stockinette st, bind off 4 (5) sts at beg of each row. **Row 3:** K 1, sl 1, k 1, psso, k across to within last 3 sts, k 2 tog, k 1. **Row 4:** P across. Rep last 2 rows 3 (4) more times —62 (66) sts. Work even in stockinette st until armholes measure 7 (7½)", end with a p row.

SHOULDERS: Bind off 5 (6) sts at beg of next 4 rows. Place rem 42 (42) sts on a st holder for back of neck.

FRONT: Work same as Back until length of armholes are 4 (4¼)", end with a p row.

NECK: K 17 (19) sts; place rem 45 (47) sts on another st holder. Working over sts on needle only, work in stockinette st, dec one st at neck edge every other row 7 times in all. Work even over rem 10 (12) sts until length of armhole is same as Back, ending at armhole edge.

SHOULDER: From armhole edge, bind off 5 (6) sts twice. Leave center 28 sts on front holder, slip rem 17 (19) sts on a No. 8 needle. Attach yarn at neck edge and work to correspond with opposite side, reversing shapings.

SLEEVES: With C and No. 5 needles, cast on 54 (58) sts. Work ribbing as for Back for 4". Break off C. Attach A. Change to No. 8 needles and with A, work in stockinette st until length is 5 (5½)" from last row of ribbing, end with a p row.

Top Shaping: Work same as for Back Armholes until Row 4 has been completed. Rep Rows 3 and 4 until 22 sts rem. Bind off 3 sts at beg of each of next 4 rows. Bind off rem 10 sts.

COLLAR: Sew left shoulder seam. With right side facing, A and No. 5 needles, k the 42 (42) sts on back holder, pick up and k 15 (17) sts along left front neck edge, k the 28 sts on front holder, pick up and k 15 (17) sts along right front neck edge—100 (104) sts. Break off A; Attach B. With B work in k 2, p 2 ribbing until collar measures 7". Bind off loosely in ribbing.

Pocket: With C and No. 5 needles, cast on 30 sts. Work in ribbing as for Back Ribbing for 4". Bind off in ribbing.

FINISHING: Block pieces to measurements. Sew side and sleeve seams. Sew right shoulder and collar seam, matching colors.

PERUVIAN HAT

MATERIALS: Bucilla Crewel Wool; 4 cards each of #39 Dark Orange (A), #31 Purple (B), #14 Med. Pink (C), #84 Peacock (D), #98 Sun Yellow (E), #85 Rosy Pink (F), #45 Dk. French Blue (G), #68 Emerald (H), #1 White (I), #12 Black (J), #47 Dk. Sage Green (K), #33 Royal Blue (L), #35 Med. Red (M). Dp Needles, 1 set of 5 No. 6 OR SIZE TO OBTAIN GAUGE. Crochet Hook, Size E.

GAUGE: 6 sts = 1″; 13 rows = 2″.

TO MAKE: With color A, cast on 116 sts, divide evenly on 4 needles—29 sts on each needle. With care not to twist sts, join and p 1 round. Break A. **Note:** When working with 2 colors twist yarns when changing colors to prevent holes and carry color not being used along wrong side of hat twisting about every 2nd or 3rd st. Do not pull carried yarn too tight. **Pat 1—Rnd 1:** Join B and p 2, join C and p 2, * with B p 2, with C p 2; repeat from * around. Following chart 1 from right to left, starting with Row 2 rep between arrows around. All remaining rounds are stockinette st (k each rnd). **Pat 2—Rnd 1:** Join D and E, k around. Follow chart 2 starting with Row 2 rep between arrows around. **Pat 3:** Follow chart 3 starting with Row 1, rep between arrows around. **Pat 4:** Follow chart 4 rep between small arrows 3 times, repeat from small arrow once more ending at large arrow for each rnd. **Pat 5:** Follow chart 5, rep in same manner as for Pat 4. **Pat 6—Rnd 1:** Join L and dec 3 sts evenly spaced on each needle—104 sts. Follow chart 6 starting with Row 2 rep between small arrows 3 times, rep from small arrow once more ending at large arrow for each rnd through rnd 6. **Rnd 7:** Work as for rnd 1—92 sts. **Pat 7—Rnd 1:** Join B and dec 3 sts evenly spaced on each needle—80 sts. Follow chart 7 starting with Row 2, rep between arrows and dec in rnd 5 same as in rnd 1—68 sts. **Pat 8—Rnd 1:** Join J, dec 3 sts evenly spaced on each needle—56 sts. Follow chart 8 starting with Row 2, rep between arrows and dec in rnd 5 same as in rnd 1, 44 sts. **Pat 9—Rnd 1:** Join H, dec 2 sts on each needle—36 sts. **Rnd 2:** With H k 1, join I k 3, * with H k 3, with I k 3; rep from * around to within last 2 sts, with H k 2. **Rnd 3:** * With I k 1, with H k 1; rep from * around. **Rnd 4:**

* With I k 2 tog., with H k 1, with I k 2, with H k 1, with I k 2 tog., with H k 1; rep from * around—28 sts. **Rnd 5:** * With I k 1, with H k 1, with I k 2 tog, with H k 1, with I k 1, with H k 1; rep from * around—24 sts. **Rnd 6:** Rep rnd 2. Break I. **Rnd 7:** With H, dec 2 sts on each needle—16 sts. Break yarn, leaving 8″ end. Thread end in tapestry needle and draw through rem sts; draw up tightly and secure.

EAR COVERS—(Make 2): Using 2 needles, with D cast on 21 sts, working in stockinette st (p 1 row, k 1 row) for 6 rows; follow chart for ear covers starting with row 3, work through row 15. **Next Row:** With D, sl 1, k 1, psso, k to within last 2 sts, k 2 tog. **Next Row:** Sl 1, p 1, psso, p to within last st, then slip the last p st from right needle back to left needle (2 sts on left needle), pass the un-worked st over the last p st then slip this remaining st back to right needle. Rep last 2 rows once. Break D. **Edge:** Right side facing, with 2nd needle and F, pick up and k 13 sts along right hand side edge of ear cover, with 3rd needle k 13 sts of ear cover, with free needle pick up and k 13 sts on left hand edge of ear cover.

Working back and forth across the 3 needles with F, k 2 rows. Break F. **Next Row:** Join B and k 3 sts, join K and k 3, * with B k 3, with

K k 3; rep from * across 3 needles, end with k 3 B. Rep last row once more. Break B & K. Join H and k 2 rows. Break H. Join A, k 1 row. Bind off **loosely.**

PICOT EDGING: With right side of hat facing and size E hook, join A at center back edge of hat, work 1 sc in each of first 3 cast-on sts, * ch 3, 1 sc in each of next 3 sts; rep from * around, ch 3, join with sl st. Work same edging around curved edge of ear covers. Attach cast-on edge of ear covers to hat, spacing each one about 2″ from center front of hat.

TIES: (Make 2 of each color combination)—With 2 strands each of H and I make a ch 4″ long. Attach one at front of each ear cover. With 2 strands each of A and I make a ch 6″ long. Attach one at back of each ear cover. Make two 8-strand tassels of D and attach at ends of white and green ties. Make two 8-strand tassels of I and attach at ends of white and orange ties. Make six 12-strand tassels of F and attach one at center lower edge of each ear cover and one at points where ties are attached.

TO MAKE TASSEL: Wind yarn around a desired length piece of cardboard. Tie one edge; cut opposite edge. Trim.

CHART 1   CHART 2   CHART 3

⊠ PURPLE   ⊠ PEACOCK   ⊠ ROSY PINK
□ MED PINK   □ SUN YELLOW   □ FRENCH BLUE

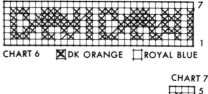

CHART 6   ⊠ DK ORANGE   □ ROYAL BLUE

CHART 4   ⊠ EMERALD   □ WHITE   ⊡ BLACK

CHART 5   ⊠ SAGE GREEN   □ MED PINK

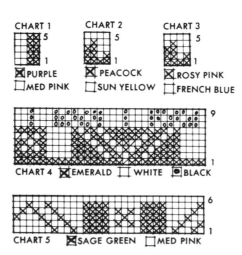

EAR COVERS

⊠ PEACOCK   □ WHITE

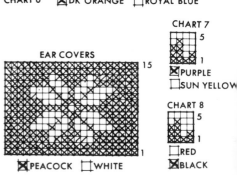

CHART 7

⊠ PURPLE
□ SUN YELLOW

CHART 8

□ RED
⊠ BLACK

SIZES: Directions are for small size (6–8). Changes for medium size (10–12) and large size (14–16) are in parentheses.

MATERIALS: Coats & Clark's "Red Heart" Wintuk Sport Yarn (2 ply 2-oz pull-out sk), 9 (10–12) skeins Camel. **For Embroidery:** Coats & Clark's "Red Heart" Wintuk (4 ply), a few yards each of Scarlet, Lt. Gold, Robin Blue and Forest Green. 6" neck zipper. Tapestry needle, size 18. 2 doz large green glossy wooden beads. Knitting Needles, 1 pair No. 6 OR SIZE TO OBTAIN GAUGE. Aluminum crochet hook, size G.

GAUGE: 6 sts = 1"; 8 rows = 1".

BLOCKING MEASUREMENTS: Bust—33 (36–40)". Width of back or front at underarm—16½ (18–20)"; at lower edge—20½ (22–24)"; width of sleeves at lower edge—18 (18¾–19½)"; at upperarm—12 (12¾–13½)".

SEED STITCH: * K 1, p 1. Repeat from * across, end k 1. Repeat row, having a k 1 over a p st, p 1 over a k st on row facing you.

BACK: Beg at lower edge, cast on 123 (131–143) sts. Work in seed st for 5 rows, inc 1 st at end of last row—124 (132–144) sts. Work in stockinette st (k 1 row, p 1 row), dec 1 st each end every 12th row 12 times—100 (108–120) sts. Work even until total length is 20 (20½–21)" or desired length to underarms, end p row. Mark last row.

ARMHOLES: Bind off 7 (8–9) sts at beg of next 2 rows. Dec 1 st each end of next row, then every other row 2 (2–4) times—80 (86–92) sts. Work even until armholes are 2 (3–3½)" above marked row, end p row.

BACK OPENING: K 40 (43–46), sl next 40 (43–46) sts on st holder. Turn and work even until armhole is 7 (8–8½)" above marked row, end at armhole edge.

SHOULDER AND NECK: Bind off 6 (7–8) sts at beg of armhole edge twice, then 6 (5–6) sts once; **at same time,** from first shoulder row, bind off 11 (12–12) sts at beg of back opening edge twice. Slip sts from holder to needle. Beg at back opening edge work other side to correspond.

FRONT: Work as for Back until armhole shaping has been completed. Work even on 80 (86–92) sts until armhole is 5½ (6½–7)" above marked row, end p row.

NECK: K 36 (38–41), place these sts on st holder, bind off loosely next 8 (10–10) sts, k remaining sts—36 (38–41) sts on needle. Work 1 row even. * Bind off 3 sts at beg of next row at neck edge and every other row 4 times more, then 3 (4, 4) sts once—18 (19–22) sts. If necessary, work even until armhole is same as back to shoulder, end at armhole edge.

SHOULDER: Bind off 6 (7–8) sts at beg of armhole edge twice, then 6 (5–6) sts once. Slip sts from holder to needle. Join yarn at neck edge and beg at * work opposite side to correspond.

SLEEVES: Beg at lower edge, cast on 107 (113–117) sts. Work in seed st for 6 rows.

Work in stockinette st for 2 (6, 6) rows. Dec one st each end of next row, then every 6th row 17 times. Work even on 71 (77–81) sts until total length is 16½ (17–17)" or desired length to underarm, end p row.

TOP SHAPING: Bind off 7 (8–9) sts at beg of next 2 rows. Dec 1 st each end of next row, then every other row 14 (16–18) times. Bind off 3 (3, 2) sts at beg of next 6 rows. Bind off remaining 9 (9–13) sts.
Block pieces. Sew shoulder seams.

NECKBAND: With right side facing, pick up and k evenly along entire neck edge 119 (123–129) sts. **Row 1:** K 1, * p 1, k 1. Rep from * across. **Row 2:** (K 1, p 1) 4 (5, 7) times; * k 2 tog, p 2 tog—2 sts decreased; (k 1, p 1) 5 times. Rep from * across, ending last repeat with (k 1, p 1) 4 (5, 6) times, k 1. **Row 3:** K 1, * p 1, k 1. Rep from * across. With a pin, mark center front of neck. **Row 4:** Working in seed st, dec 2 sts in line with each shoulder seam, and 2 sts 1½ inches before and 1½ inches beyond center front marker—8 sts decreased. **Rows 5, 6 and 7:** Rep rows 3, 4, and 3.

FRONT FRINGE: Make a row of basting sts across Front 1" below armhole shaping. Cut a 7" square of cardboard. Working with 2 strands of yarn held tog and with neck toward you, insert crochet hook under first knit st on basted line at armhole edge and draw a lp through, ch 1, * holding cardboard close to basting line, wind yarn over and around cardboard, insert hook under next st along basted line and draw a lp through, yo hook and draw through both lps on hook—lp st made. Rep from * across, moving cardboard

along when crowded. Cut lps at folds to form fringe; trim evenly. Make fringe in same way along armhole edges of Front.

RIGHT SLEEVE FRINGE: With a pin, mark center top edge of one Sleeve and place another pin on lower edge, 5" from left side edge. Make a diagonal row of basting sts from pin to pin. Beg at top edge, make fringe along the basting line, as before. For Left Sleeve fringe, place pin on lower edge 5" from right side edge. Make basting line from pin to pin and beg at lower edge, make fringe as before.
Sew side and sleeve seams. Sew in sleeves. Holding lower edge of Tunic away from you, make fringe in each st of the cast-on sts on front and back. Sew in zipper.

EMBROIDERY: With basting thread, make a row of basting up from midpoint to neckband. From point at which basting hits top of neckband mark off 5½" on either side (11" across). Starting ¼" up from front fringe of bodice at center basting line, run basting out 2⁵⁄₁₆" on each side (4⅝" across). Now connect points diagonally as on diagram. Following diagram and color key, embroider design in Satin Stitch. Make 3 couching sts evenly spaced on the longest sts of the diamond motif and 1 couching st in the center of the longest st below the diamond motif. Working across the upper front fringe and spacing 7 beads evenly across, draw 12 strands of fringe through each bead, and push bead close to base of fringe. Using 8 beads for each sleeve, string beads onto sleeve fringe in same way.

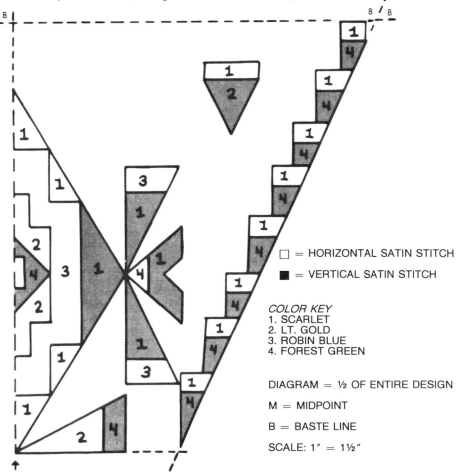

□ = HORIZONTAL SATIN STITCH

■ = VERTICAL SATIN STITCH

COLOR KEY
1. SCARLET
2. LT. GOLD
3. ROBIN BLUE
4. FOREST GREEN

DIAGRAM = ½ OF ENTIRE DESIGN

M = MIDPOINT

B = BASTE LINE

SCALE: 1" = 1½"

NOMAD'S VEST

SIZES: Directions are for size 10. Changes for sizes 12, 14 and 16 are in parentheses.

MATERIALS: Lopi (100-gr skn): 6 (7–8–9) skns. Knitting Needles, 1 Pair No. 10½—10-inch length OR SIZE TO OBTAIN GAUGE. Steel Crochet Hook, No. 00 (dble zero). 8 (½″) bone rings. One piece of cardboard 2¾″ × 12″.

GAUGE: 3 sts = 1″; 6 rows = 1½″.

BLOCKING MEASUREMENTS: Width of back at underarm—17 (18–19–20)″. Width of each front at underarm—9 (10–10½–11)″.

BACK: Starting at lower edge, cast on 52 (54–56–60) sts. **Row 1:** Purl. **Row 2:** Knit. **Row 3:** K 2, hold cardboard in back of work, * insert needle into next st as if to k, bring yarn down between work and cardboard and back up around the 2¾″ width of cardboard, yo and draw loop through st but do not sl st off left-hand needle, place st just made on left-hand needle, then k 2 tog through back of sts and sl both sts off left-hand needle to complete loop st; rep from * across to last st, k last st. **Row 4:** K in back of each st across. **Row 5:** Purl. **Row 6:** Knit. Rep these 6 rows for pat. Work in pat until length is about 20 (20–21½–21½)″, ending with a loop st row.

ARMHOLES: Continuing in pat throughout, bind off 4 (4–5–5) sts at beg of next 2 rows. Dec one st at each end every other row 4 (4–4–5) times—36 (38–38–40) sts. Work even in pat until armholes measure 7 (7½–8–8½)″. Bind off.

LEFT FRONT: Cast on 28 (30–32–34) sts. Work as for Back to armholes, ending with a loop st row.

ARMHOLE AND NECK: Working in pat, bind off 4 (4–5–5) sts at beg of next row. Dec one st at each end of every other row 4 (4–4–5) times—16 (18–19–19) sts. Keeping armhole straight, continue to dec one st at neck edge every other row 6 (6–7–7) times—10 (12–12–12) sts. Work even until armhole measures same as on Back. Bind off.

RIGHT FRONT: Work to correspond with Left Front, reversing shaping.

FINISHING: Lightly steam pieces to measurements. DO NOT PRESS. Sew shoulder and side seams. With right side facing, starting at right lower corner, sc in end st of every other row along right front edge, putting in a bone ring on every 3rd fringe row 4 times (to do this, hold ring behind work and sc through st and ring at the same time). Continue to sc along right front edge to shoulder seam; sc in each st across back of neck; then work along left front edge to correspond with opposite edge, putting rings in line with rings on right front; 3 sc in corner st; sc in each st across entire lower edge, 3 sc in next corner st. Join with sl st to first sc. Ch 1, * sc in each sc on last rnd to within next ring, turn ring with free edge in line with last sc, sc in ring only, skip next sc to complete eyelet; rep from * 7 more times; sc in each rem sc. Join. Break off and fasten. Work 2 rnds of sc along each armhole.

CORD: Make a chain the desired length. Lace cord through eyelets.

SIZES: Directions are for small size (8-10). Changes for medium (12-14) and large (16-18) sizes are in parentheses.

MATERIALS: Reynolds Lopi — 100% mountain sheep's wool (100-gr or 3.6-oz skns); 5 (5-6) skns main color (MC); 1 skn contrasting color (CC). Circular Knitting Needles, 1 each Nos. 9 and 13 OR SIZE TO OBTAIN GAUGE. Crochet Hook, Size J. 2 large ornamental hooks and eyes. 3 large st holders.

GAUGE: On No. 13 needle—7 sts = 2".

FINISHED MEASUREMENTS: Bust — 37½ (41-44½)"; width of back at underarm—18¾ (20½-22¼)"; width of sleeve at upper arm—13½ (14½-15½)".

Start at lower edge with MC and No. 9 needle, cast on 114 (122-130) sts. Being careful not to twist sts, join. Work in rnds of k 1, p 1 ribbing for 2½". Mark end of rnds. **Next Rnd:** K around, increasing one st every 7th (6th-5th) st—130 (142-156) sts. Change to No. 13 needle.

BODY: Rnd 1: *With yarn in back, sl 1, k 1; rep from * around. **Rnd 2:** *K 1, with yarn in back sl 1; rep from * around. **For Medium Size Only,** inc one st at end of last rnd to get 143 sts. **For All Sizes: Attach CC. Note: Design is worked en-entirely in st st (k each rnd). Carry color not in use loosely along wrong side of work; always pick up new color from under other strand. When one color is carried across 4 or more sts, twist color not in use around other strand once every 4th st to hold in place.** Work design from Chart as follows: Follow each row on Chart from A to D, knitting every st; rep from A to D around; inc one st **on Small and Large Sizes Only** at end of last rnd—131 (143-157) sts. **For All Sizes:** Break off CC. **Next Rnd:** With yarn in back sl 1, *k 1, sl 1; rep from * around. **Next Rnd:** K 1, *sl 1, k 1; rep from * around. Rep last 2 Rnds alternately for pat until total length is 12" from beg, end with 2nd Rnd of pat.

KEY:

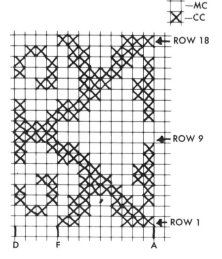

☐ —MC
☒ —CC

← ROW 18
← ROW 9
← ROW 1

D   F   A

Front Opening: Next Rnd: Work in pat across 93 (103-113) sts; bind off 8 sts; being careful to keep in pat, work to end of rnd and continue across to within bound-off sts. Turn. Now work back and forth in rows as follows: **Row 1 (wrong side):** P every slipped st and with yarn in front sl every knitted st on previous rnd. Turn. **Row 2:** Work in pat across—123 (135-149) sts. Rep last 2 rows alternately until length is 17" from beg, end with a right-side row.

ARMHOLES: Next Row: Work in pat over 27 (29-33) sts for left front; place these sts on a st holder; bind off loosely next 6 (8-10) sts for underarm; work in pat until there are 57 (61-63) sts on right-hand point of needle, from bound-off sts, for back; place back sts on a separate large st holder; bind off loosely next 6 (8-10) sts for underarm; complete row in pat for right front; place these 27 (29-33) sts on a separate st holder. Break off yarn. Put aside and start sleeves.

SLEEVES: With MC and No. 9 needle, cast on 26 (28-30) sts. Do not join. Work back and forth in rows of k 1, p 1 ribbing for 3½". **Next row (wrong side):** P across, increasing 9 (7-9) sts evenly spaced across row — 35 (35-39) sts. Change to No. 13 needle and work pat as follows: **Row 1 (right side):** K 1, *with yarn in back sl 1, k 1; rep from * across. **Row 2:** With yarn in front sl 1, *p 1, with yarn in front sl 1; rep from * across. Attach CC and work design from Chart as follows: Design is worked in rows of st st (k 1 row, p 1 row), carry color not in use loosely along wrong side of work. For all k rows, follow Chart from A to D twice, then from A to E (E-D) once more; for all p rows, follow from E (E-D) to A once, then from D to A twice. Follow Chart in this manner. When design has been completed, break off CC. With MC, rep Rows 1 and 2 of sleeve pat once; then keeping continuity of pat, inc one st at each end of next row and every 4th row thereafter until there are 47 (51-55) sts. Work even in pat until total length is about 17 (17½-18)" from beg, end with a wrong-side row. Keeping in pat, bind off 3 (4-5) sts at beg of next 2 rows — 41 (43-45) sts. Break off yarn. Place these sts on No. 9 needle. Work other Sleeve in same way. Break off yarn and place sts on same No. 9 needle. Now join for Raglan Shaping as follows: **Row 1:** With right side of all sections facing, using No. 13 needle and keeping continuity of pat across each section, work across Right Front sts, place a marker on needle; continuing with same skn of yarn, work across one sleeve, place a marker on needle; work across back sts, place a marker on needle; work across other sleeve, place a marker on needle; work across left front sts—193 (205-219) sts. **Row 2:** Keeping in pat across each section and slipping markers, work across all sts. **Row 3:** *Work in pat to within 2 sts before next marker, k 2 tog, sl marker, sl 1, k 1, psso; rep from * 3 more times; complete row—dec made before and after each marker. **Rows 4 through 10:** Rep last 2 rows three times, then rep Row 2 once more—161 (173-187) sts. Attach CC for design. **Next Row:** Working in rows of st st, follow 1st Row on Chart from A to D; rep A to D until 2 sts before next marker, continuing design, k 2 tog, sl marker; starting at A on Chart after each marker and making decs before and after each marker, continue in this manner across each section. Continuing decs before and after each marker on every right-side row and keeping continuity of design over each section (including dec sts), follow Chart back and forth through Row 9 only. **At same time,** dec one st at each end of needle for neck shaping on 2nd row of design and every 7th (5th-4th) row thereafter to top. After design has been completed, break off CC. With MC, continue in pat making raglan and neck decs as directed until 3 sts rem on each sleeve. Bind off loosely rem sts, decreasing one st at beg and end of needle.

Shawl Collar: Start at base of front opening with MC and No. 13 needle, cast on 8 sts. Work in rows of garter st (k each row) for 7". **Next row:** Inc one st in first st, mark this edge for inner edge of collar; k across. Continue in garter st, increasing one st at inner edge every other row until there are 28 sts on needle. Mark last inc made at inner edge. Work even in garter st for 3 (3¼-3½)" from last marker, ending at outer edge (straight edge of collar). Work short rows as follows: **Row 1:** From outer edge, k 7, turn. **Row 2:** Sl 1, k to end. **Row 3:** K 14, turn. **Row 4:** Sl 1, k to end. **Row 5:** K 21, turn. **Row 6:** Sl 1, k to end. **Row 7:** K 28, turn. **Row 8:** Rep Row 6. Rep Rows 5, 4, 3, 2 and 1; then rep Row 2 once more. Work in garter st across all sts until length from last marker on inner edge is 6 (6½-7)". Continuing in garter st, dec one st at inner edge every other row until 8 sts rem. Work even over 8 sts for 7". Bind off.

FINISHING: Steam very lightly from wrong side. Baste collar to front opening and neck edge, adjusting to fit; overlap right front over left front at base of front opening and baste double edge to bound-off sts at center front. **To Join:** With right side facing, hold MC to wrong side of work; with crochet hook, draw up a lp at beg of left side seam of front opening; holding yarn on wrong side, sl st in edge of garter st band of collar, *working along basting, sl st in edge of sweater ¼" above last st, sl st in edge of collar, ¼" above last st made; rep from * along entire inner edge of collar and across base of front opening. Break off and fasten. Remove basting. Sew sleeve and underarm seams. Fasten front opening with 2 hooks and eyes, having first one at beg of neck shaping and the other at center of opening.

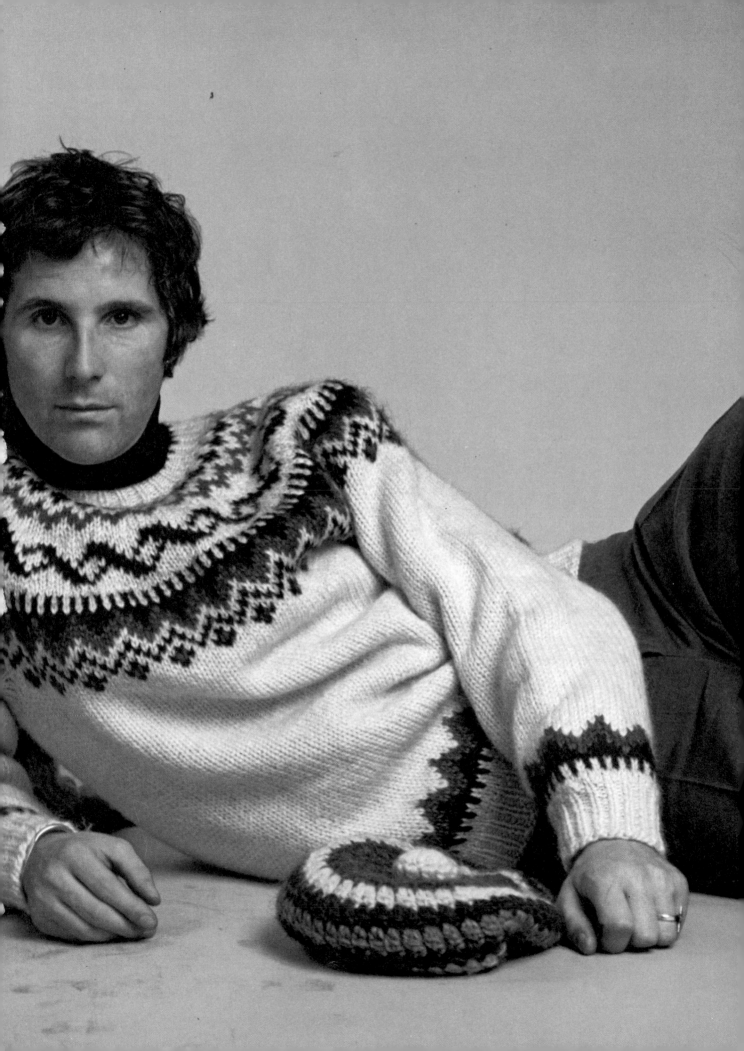

Directions are for bust or chest size 30-32". Changes for sizes 34-36", 38-40" and 42-44" are in parentheses.

MATERIALS: Reynolds Lopi, pure wool, (3.6-oz skn), natural colors: 6 (7-8-9) skns #51, white (A), 1 skn each #52 black (B) and #53 brown (C). Circular knitting needles, 1 pair each of Nos. 6 and 10 (29" long) OR SIZE TO OBTAIN GAUGE. One set each of double-pointed needles, Nos. 6 and 10 (14" long). Crochet Hook, Size G. 2 large st holders.

GAUGE: On No. 10 needle—7 sts = 2"; 5 rows = 1".

FINISHED MEASUREMENTS: Bust or Chest—36 (39-43-46)", width of sleeve at upper arm—14 (15-16-17)".

Note: Body and lower section of Yoke are worked in rnds on circular needles. Sleeves and top section of Yoke are worked in rnds on dp needles.

BODY: Start at lower edge with A and No. 6 circular needle, cast on 100 (114-124-138) sts. Being careful not to twist sts, join. Mark end of rnds. Work in rnds of k 1, p 1 ribbing for 2". Now work in st st (k each rnd) as follows: **Rnd 1:** Continuing with A, inc one st in first st, k 2 (2-2-4), inc in next st, *k 3 (4-4-5); inc in next st; rep from * around —126 (138-150-162) sts. **Rnd 2:** K around. **Border Pattern:** Change to No. 10 needle; attach B and C. **Note: When changing color always twist color not in use around the other to prevent making holes in work. Carry color not in use loosely along wrong side of work.** Continuing in rnds of st st, follow Chart 1 to end of last row. Break off B and C. With A, work even in st st until total length is 15 (15-15½-16)". Divide sts as follows: **Next Rnd:** With A, k 53 (59-65-71) for Back and place these sts on a st holder; bind off next 10 sts for underarm; k until there are on right-hand point of needle 53 (59-65-71) sts for Front and place these sts on a separate holder; bind off rem 10 sts for underarm. Break off yarn. Put aside.

SLEEVES: With A and 2 dp needles No. 6, cast on 28 (32-34-36) sts. Divide sts on 3 dp needles and being careful not

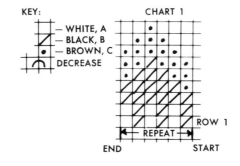

KEY:
— WHITE, A
— BLACK, B
— BROWN, C
— DECREASE

CHART 1
ROW 1
REPEAT
END   START

CHART 2
ROW 1
REPEAT
END   START

CHART 3
ROW 1
REPEAT
END   START

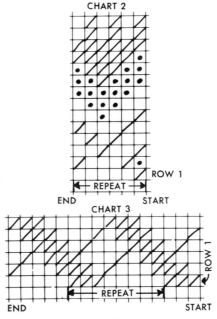

to twist sts, join. Mark end of rnds. Work in rnds of k 1, p 1 ribbing for 2". **Next Rnd:** K, increasing 8 (10-14-12) sts evenly spaced around—36 (42-48-48) sts. **Next Rnd:** K around. **Border Pattern:** Change to No. 10 dp needles. Follow Chart 1 to end of last row, working in rnds of st st (k each rnd) as for Body. Break off B and C. With A, continuing in st st, inc one st at beg and end of every 8th (10th-12th-10th) rnd 7 (5-4-5) times—50 (52-56-58) sts. Work even until total length is 15½ (16-16½-17)". **Next Rnd:** K to within last 5 sts of rnd; bind off next 10 (9-10-9) sts for underarm. Place rem 40 (43-46-49) sts on a contrasting colored strand of yarn.

Break off A. Work other sleeve in same way.

Yoke: With right side facing, place sts on No. 10 (29") needle in the following order: Back, one Sleeve, Front and other Sleeve — 186 (204-222-240) sts. With A, work in stockinette st for 2 (2-4-4) rnds. **Yoke Pattern:** Follow Chart 2 to end of last row. **Next Rnd:** With A only, k around. **Next (Dec) Rnd:** With A, k 4 (9, 1, 0), *(k 1, k 2 tog) 3 (3, 3, 1) times; k 2, k 2 tog) 1 (1, 1, 3) times; rep from * around—130 (144, 164, 184) sts. **Next Row:** With A, k around, decreasing 2 (0, 4, 8) sts evenly spaced around—128 (144-160-176) sts. Now follow Chart 3 to end of last row. With A, k around. Change to the dp needles No. 10. **Next (Dec) Rnd:** With A, (k 1,

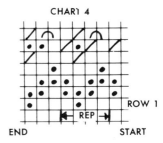

CHART 4
ROW 1
REP
END   START

k 2 tog) 1 (9-17-25) times; (k 2, k 2 tog) 16 (12-8-4) times; (k 1, k 2 tog) 0 (8-16-24) times; (k 2, k 2 tog) 15 (11-7-3) times; k 1—96 (104-112-120) sts. With A, k around. Follow Chart 4 to end of Row 6. Follow Row 7 on Chart 4 making 24 (26-28-30) decs evenly spaced around as indicated on Chart—72 (78-84-90) sts. With A, k 1 rnd even. **Next Rnd:** K around, decreasing 20 (24-26-28) sts evenly around — 52 (54-58-62) sts.

Neckband: Change to dp No. 6 needles and with A, work in k 1, p 1 ribbing for 1". Bind off loosely in ribbing.

FINISHING: Weave bound-off sts at underarms tog. To block, place pullover on a padded surface, adjust to measurements; cover with a damp cloth and allow to dry; **do not press.** With B and crochet hook, sc evenly along neck edge, allowing for stretching. Join with sl st to first sc. Break off and fasten.

TARTAN PLAID SKIRT

SIZES: Directions are for small size (6-8). Changes for medium (10-12) and large (14-16) sizes are in parentheses.

MATERIALS: Columbia—Minerva Nantuk, 4-ply acrylic yarn (4 oz skn): 5 (6-6) skns Scarlet (S); 2 skns each Kelly Green (G) and Imperial Blue (Bl); 1 skn each Black (B) and White (W). Knitting Needles, 1 pair No. 8 OR SIZE TO OBTAIN GAUGE. Crochet Hook, Size G. 1 yd elastic, ³⁄₈" wide. A few yards binding tape.

NOTE: 4-ply Nantuk is used interchangeably with Columbia-Minerva's knitting worsted.

GAUGE: 9 sts = 2"; 6 rows = 1".

BLOCKING MEASUREMENTS: Waist (without elastic)—28 (30-33)". Width of each panel at top edge 7 (7½-8¼)". Width of each panel at hipline—10 (11-12)".

Note: Skirt is knitted in 4 panels of diagonal stripes. The crossing B and W stripes are crocheted later on, after knitting has been completed.

STRIPE PAT: Working in stockinette st (k 1 row, p 1 row), make * 2 rows B; 12 rows S; 5 rows Bl; 2 rows W; 5 rows G; 2 rows B; 5 rows G; 2 rows W; 5 rows Bl; 12 rows S—52 rows in all; rep from * for stripe pat throughout. Carry unused color loosely along side of work over B stripes only. Break off at end of all other stripes and attach next color.

BACK: Right Panel: Start at upper right corner with S, cast on 3 sts. **Rows 1-2-3:** Working in stockinette st (k 1 row, p 1 row), inc one st at both ends of every row—9 sts. **Row 4:** Inc one st at beg of row (mark beg of row to indicate side edge of panel); p rem sts—**inc made at side edge only.** End of this row is at waist edge of skirt. Drop S; attach B. Starting at *, work in the Stripe Pat as directed, continuing to inc one st at both ends of each of 3 rows and inc one st at side edge only on following row until there are 66 (70-75) sts. Mark st at top edge of last row to indicate beg of center back seam. Continue to inc one st at side edge on every row as before, **at the same time,** dec one st at opposite edge (center back edge) on every other row until there are 105 (109-114) sts and total length at side edge is about 40 (40½-41)".

Hemline Shaping: Continue to dec one st at center back edge every other row as before; **at the same time,** shape opposite edge for hemline as follows: * Dec one st at hemline edge on each of next 3 rows, then work one row even; continuing center back decs, rep from * until 3 or 2 sts rem. Work rem sts tog; break off and fasten.

Left Panel: Start at upper left corner with S, cast on 3 sts. **Rows 1-2-3:** Working in stockinette st, inc one st at both ends of each row. **Row 4:** P across, inc one st at end of row (mark end of row as side edge). Beg of last row is at top edge of panel. Complete same as Right Panel.

Crossing Stripes: With right side facing and waist edge of right panel toward you, counting from marker at beg of center back edge, attach B between 9th and 10th sts on waist edge. Hold yarn on wrong side and with crochet hook on right side, working up in a straight line, sl st in strand between sts over each row to outer edge, being careful not to pull in work—**B stripe made.** Break off and fasten. * Sk 9 sts from last stripe made, attach W to strand between last st skipped and next st on waist edge and with W, work sl st stripe between sts same as B stripe. Break off and fasten. Having 2 sts between stripes, make another B and another W stripe in the same manner. Sk 9 sts from last stripe and starting at side edge, if necessary, make one B stripe. Hereafter start each stripe at side edge; rep from * throughout panel. Work sl st stripes on left panel to correspond with right panel. Sew center back seam.

FRONT: Work same as Back, making Left Panel same as Right Panel and Right Panel same as Left Panel of Back.

FINISHING: To block pieces made with acrylic yarn, pin to measurements on a padded surface. Cover with damp cloth and allow to dry (do not press). Sew side seams. With S, sc evenly along top edge. Join to first sc. Break off. Cut elastic the desired length, allowing ½" for sewing; overlap ends for ½" and sew. Fold ½" of top of skirt to wrong side for casing, inserting circle of elastic, sew in place. Sew tape along lower edge; turn a ³⁄₄" hem (or wider if desired) and stitch in place.

RED TURTLENECK HALTER TOP

SIZES: Directions are for small size (6-8). Changes for medium (10-12) and large (14-16) sizes are in parentheses.

MATERIALS: Columbia—Minerva Nantuk 4-ply acrylic yarn (4 oz skn): 1½ (2-2) skns Red. Knitting Needles, 1 pair each Nos. 6 and 8 OR SIZE TO OBTAIN GAUGE.

GAUGE: 9 sts = 2"; 6 rows = 1".

BLOCKING MEASUREMENTS: Bust—31 (34-38)". Width of back or front at underarms—15½ (17-19)". Length at center front, excluding collar—13¼ (14½-15½)".

BACK: Start at lower edge with No. 6 needles, cast on 68 (76-84) sts. Work in k 1, p 1 ribbing for 1½". Change to No. 8 needles and work in stockinette st (k 1 row, p 1 row) until total length is 7½ (8-8½)", ending with a p row. Place sts on a stitch holder. Break off yarn.

FRONT: Work same as Back but retain sts on needle; do not break off.

Top Raglan Shaping: Row 1: K 1, sl 1, k 1, psso, k across row to within last 3 sts, k 2 tog, k 1—dec made at each end. **Row 2:** P across. Rep last 2 rows alternately 16 (18-20) more times—34 (38-42) sts.

NECK: Row 1: K 1, sl 1, k 1, psso, k 9 (9-11); place rem 22 (26-28) sts on another stitch holder. **Row 2:** Working over sts on needle only, bind off 3 (3-4) sts, p across. **Row 3:** K 1, sl 1, k 1, psso, k across. **Rows 4-5:** Rep last 2 rows. **Row 6:** P across. Bind off rem 3 sts. Leaving center 10 (14-14) sts on front holder, place rem 12 (12-14) sts on a No. 8 needle; attach yarn at neck edge and k across, decreasing at end of row as before. Work to correspond with opposite side, reversing shaping. Sew side seams.

Ribbed Band: With right side facing and No. 6 needles, pick up and k 39 (42-44) sts along right edge of front raglan shaping, k sts on back holder, pick up and k 40 (42-44) sts along left edge of raglan shaping—146 (160-172) sts. Work in k 1, p 1 ribbing for ½". Bind off ribbing.

Collar: With right side facing and No. 6 needles, starting and ending at end of last row of ribbed band, pick up and k 44 (48-52) sts evenly along front neck edge, including sts on front holder; cast on 32 sts for back of neck—76 (80-84) sts. Work in k 1, p 1 ribbing for 4½". Bind off loosely in ribbing. Sew collar seam. Fold collar in half to right side.

SLEEVELESS V NECK PULLOVER

SIZES: Directions are for small (6-8) size. Changes for medium (10-12) and large (14-16) sizes are in parentheses.

MATERIALS: Coats & Clark's Red Heart "Wintuk" 2 Ply Sport yarn (2 oz skn): 3 (4—4) ozs 12 Black (B), 2 ozs each 902 Red (R) and 648 Apple Green (G). Knitting Needles, 1 pair No. 6 OR SIZE TO OBTAIN GAUGE.

GAUGE: Stockinette st—6 sts = 1"; 8 rows = 1".

BLOCKING MEASUREMENTS: Bust—32½ (35-39)". Width of back at under-arm—16¼ (17½-19½)".

BACK: Start at lower edge with R, cast on 97 (105-117) sts. **Row 1:** K 1, * p 1, k 1; rep from * across. **Row 2:** P 1, * k 1, p 1; rep from * across. Rep last 2 rows alternately for ribbing. Work in ribbing until 8 rows in all have been made. Break off R; attach G. **Next 8 rows:** With G, k 1 row, then work 7 rows in ribbing as established. Break off G; attach Red. Working as for last 8 rows, continue to work stripes as follows: 8 rows R; 8 rows B; 8 rows R; 8 rows G and 8 rows R. Now with Black only, work in stockinette st (k 1 row, p 1 row) until total

length is 12 (12½-13)", end with a p row.

ARMHOLES: Row 1: *K 1, sl 1, k 1, psso* —**dec made at beg of row;** k across up to last 3 sts, *k 2 tog, k 1*—**dec made at end of row. Row 2:** P across. Rep last 2 rows alternately until 37 (37-41) sts rem. For Shoulders, bind off 2 sts at beg of next 2 rows. Place rem 33 (33-37) sts on a stitch holder.

FRONT: Work same as Back until total length is 10 (10½-11)", end with a p row.

continued on page 90

SLEEVELESS V NECK PULLOVER continued from page 87

NECK: Row 1: K 48 (52-58), place these sts just worked on a stitch holder; bind off next st; k rem sts—48 (52-58) sts on needle. **Row 2:** Working over sts on needle only, p across. **Row 3:** *K 2 tog—* **dec made at neck edge;** complete row. Continuing in stockinette st, dec one st at neck edge every 6th row 2 more times, end last row at side edge—45 (49-55) sts.

ARMHOLES: Continue to dec one st at neck edge every 6th row 3 (7-7) more times, then dec at same edge every 4th row 10 (6-8) times, **AT THE SAME TIME,** at side edge, (making decs as for Back Armholes), dec one st at beg of next row and every other row thereafter 30 (34-38) times in all. Bind off rem 2 sts

for Shoulder. Slip sts from front holder onto a needle, attach B to neck edge and work to correspond with opposite side, reversing shaping.

FINISHING: To block, pin back and front to measurements on a padded surface; cover with a damp cloth and allow to dry (do not press). Sew left shoulder seam. **Neckband:** With right side facing, using G, k across sts on back stitch holder, pick up and k 56 (62-68) sts along front left side edge of neck, place a marker on needle; pick up and k one st at center front, place a marker on needle; pick up and k 56 (62-68) sts along front right side edge of neck—146 (158-174) sts. **Row 1 (wrong side):** Work in p 1, k 1 ribbing across to

within 2 sts before next marker, p 2 tog, slip marker, k 1, slip marker, p 2 tog, work in k 1, p 1 ribbing across, end with k 1. **Row 2:** Work in p 1, k 1 ribbing across to within 2 sts before next marker, k 2 tog, slip marker, p 1, slip marker, k 2 tog; complete row in ribbing as established. Rep last 2 rows alternately until neckband measures 1". Bind off in ribbing, decreasing one st at each side of center front st. Sew right shoulder seam, including neckband. **Armhole Bands:** With right side facing, using R, pick up and k 96 (102-110) sts evenly along entire armhole edge. Work in k 1, p 1 ribbing for ³/₄". Bind off tightly in ribbing. Work other armhole band in same way. Sew side seams, including armhole bands.

CHEVRON-STITCH SKIRT AND MATCHING TOP

SIZES: Directions are for size 8. Changes for sizes 10, 12 and 14 are in parentheses.

MATERIALS: Coats & Clark's Red Heart "Wintuk" Variegated Sport Yarn — 100% Orlon® acrylic (1¾-oz Skns): 21 (23-25-27) ozs of #934 Buckie. Knitting Needles, 1 pair No. 6 OR SIZE TO OBTAIN GAUGE. Steel Crochet Hook, No. 1. One yd of ½" elastic.

GAUGE: St St — 5 sts = 1"; 7 rows = 1". Pat — 12 sts = 2"; 7 rows = 1".

FINISHED MEASUREMENTS: Top: Bust — 31½ (32½-34-36)"; width of back or front at underarm — 15¾ (16¼-17-18)"; width of sleeve at upper arm — 11½ (12-12½-13)". **Skirt:** Width of back or front at lower edge — 28 (30-32-34)"; width of back or front at top edge skirt (without elastic) — 17½ (18¾-20-21)".

SKIRT: BACK: Starting at lower edge, cast on loosely 169 (181-193-205) sts and p one row. **Row 1 (right side):** * K 1, **pick up and k one stitch between last st used and next st — one st increased;** k 4, sl 1, k 2 tog, psso — 2 sts decreased **for center of scallop;** k 4, pick up and k one st between last st used and next st as before (always inc in this manner); rep from * across, end with k 1—14 (15-16-17) scallops started. **Row 2:** P across — same number of sts as before. Rep Rows 1-2 alternately for pat. Work in pat until total length is 11"; end with a p row. Work dec rows as follows: **Dec**

Row 1: * K 1, inc one st as before, k 2, **sl 1, k 1, psso — dec made before center st of scallop;** sl 1, k 2 tog, psso, **k 2 tog — dec made after center st;** k 2, inc one st as before, **k 1 — this is single st between scallops;** inc one st, k 4, sl 1, k 2 tog, psso, k 4, inc one st; rep from * across to within last st, k 1 — one st decreased at each side of center st on first and every other scallop across. **Next Row:** P across — 155 (165-177-187) sts. **Following Row:** * K 1, inc one st, k across to within 3 center sts of same scallop, sl 1, k 2 tog, psso, k to within next single st between scallops, inc one st; rep from * across to within last st, k 1. Rep last 2 rows alternately until total length is 18", end with a p row. **Dec Row 2:** * K 1, inc one st, k to within center 3 sts of same scallop, sl 1, k 2 tog, psso, k to within next single st between scallops, inc one st, k 1, inc one st, k to within center 7 sts of scallop, sl 1, k 1, psso, sl 1, k 2 tog, psso, k 2 tog, k to within next single st between scallops, inc one st; rep from * across to within last st, k 1 — one st decreased at each side of center st on 2nd and every other scallop across. **Next Row:** P across — 141 (151-161-171) sts. Keeping in pattern throughout, work even until total length is 25"; end with a p row. **Dec Row 3:** Keeping in pattern, dec one st before and after center st on first and every other scallop across—127 (135-145-153) sts. Work even until total length is 32", ending with a p row. **Dec Row 4:** Rep

Dec Row 2—113 (121-129-137) sts. Work even over rem sts until total length is 38 (38–39–39)", end with a p row. **Note:** One inch is allowed in the length for stretching when blocking. Bind off.

FRONT: Work same as Back.

FINISHING: To block, pin pieces to measurements on a padded surface; cover with a damp cloth and allow to dry; **do not press.** Sew side seams. **Top Edging:** With right side facing, using crochet hook, attach yarn to top end of a side seam, sc evenly along top edge, skipping center st of each scallop around. Join with sl st to first sc. Break off and fasten. **Bottom Edging:** With right side facing and crochet hook attach yarn to lower end of a side seam, working along cast-on edge, sc evenly along lower edge, making sc, ch 1 and sc in center st of each scallop and making sl st in each single st between scallops. Join to first sc. Break off and fasten. **Casing:** Thread a tapestry needle with a long strand of yarn, and make casing as shown in Diagram. Insert elastic inside casing, adjust to desired length and, allowing ½" for overlap, cut. Overlap ends and sew tog.

continued on page 94

CHEVRON-STITCH SKIRT AND MATCHING TOP continued from page 91

TOP BACK: Starting at inner edge of hem, cast on 79 (81-85-90) sts. Work in st st (k 1 row, p 1 row) for 5 rows for hem, end with a k row. From wrong side, k next row for hemline. Starting with a k row, continue in st st until length is 12½ (13-13-13½)" from hemline; end with a p row.

ARMHOLES: Continuing in st st throughout, bind off 5 (5-6-6) sts at beg of next 2 rows. Dec one st each end every other row 4 times — 61 (63-65-70) sts. Work even until 5 (5½-6-6½)" from first row of armholes, ending with a p row.

NECK: K 24 (24-25-26) sts, place rem 37 (39-40-44) sts on a st holder. Working over set of sts on needle only, bind off 3 sts at neck edge at beg of next row and every other row thereafter 3 times in all; then dec one st at same edge every row 3 times, ending at armhole edge — 12 (12-13-14) sts. Work even, if necessary, until length from first row of armholes is 6½ (7-7½-8)", end at armhole edge.

SHOULDERS: Row 1: From armhole edge, bind off 6 sts; complete row. **Row 2:** P across. Bind off 6 (6-7-8) sts. Leaving center 13 (15-15-18) sts on st holder, sl rem 24 (24-25-26) sts onto a needle; attach yarn at neck edge and work to correspond with opposite side, reversing shaping.

FRONT: Work same as for Back until 2½ (3-3½-4)" from first row of armholes, end with a p row — 61 (63-65-70) sts.

NECK: Work same as for Back Neck; then work even over rem 12 (12-13-14) sts until length of armhole is same as on Back, end at armhole edge. Shape Shoulder and complete other side same as for Back.

SLEEVES: Starting at inner edge of hem, cast on 37 (41-43-45) sts. Work same as for Back until 2 (2-2½-2½)" from hemline, end with a p row. Continuing in st st, inc one st at each end of next row and every 10th row thereafter 10 times in all — 57 (61-63-65) sts. Work even until total length is 17 (17-17½-18)", end with a p row.

Top Shaping: Continuing in st st throughout, bind off 5 (5-6-6) sts at beg of next 2 rows. Work 0 (0-4-6) rows even. Dec one st at each end every other row until 17 (19-19-19) sts rem. Bind off 2 sts at beg of next 4 rows. Bind off.

FINISHING: To block, pin pieces to measurements on a padded surface, cover with a damp cloth and allow to dry; **do not press.** Sew side and sleeve seams. Sew right shoulder seam.

Neck Facing: With right side facing, starting at left shoulder, pick up and k 32 (34-34-35) sts along left front neck edge, k sts on front holder, pick up and k 32 (34-34-35) sts along right front neck edge to next shoulder seam, pick up and k 18 (18-20-20) sts along right back neck edge, k sts on back holder, pick up and k 18 (18-20-20) sts along left back neck edge — 126 (134-138-146) sts. **Row 1 (wrong side):** K across for fold ridge. **Row 2:** K across, inc 10 sts evenly spaced across row — 136 (144-148-156) sts. **Row 3:** P across. **Rows 4-5:** K 1 row, p 1 row. Bind off loosely. Sew left shoulder seam, including facing. Turn facing at fold ridge and hems at hemlines to wrong side and stitch in place. Sew in sleeves.

INDIAN AFGHAN

SIZE: Approx. 50" x 62", excluding fringe.

MATERIALS: Brunswick Germantown Knitting Worsted, 100% wool (4-oz. skns): 3 skns #486 Brew Brown (A), 2 skns #474 Brick (B), 3 skns #476 Straw (C), 4 skns #457 Cranberry (D). Knitting Needles, 1 pair No 8 OR SIZE TO OBTAIN GAUGE. Crochet Hook, Size G.

GAUGE: 5 sts = 1"; 6 rows = 1".

Note: When changing color, always twist color not in use around the other to prevent making holes in work. Use separate bobbins or separate skns for each section; do not carry color not in use along wrong side. Strips are worked in st st (k 1 row, p 1 row). Read chart from right to left for knit row, and left to right for purl row; all purl stitches are same as previous row. Read all charts from bottom up.

STRIP 1 (Make 2): With D, cast on 44 sts and follow first row on Chart for Strip 1 (each square on chart indicates one st) from right to left. Continue to follow Chart back and forth to end of last row—34 rows in all. Rep first through 34th rows 10 more times. At end of last rep, with D, bind off.

STRIP 2 (Make 3): With D, cast on 22 sts and follow Chart for Strip 2 from first row to end of last row—34 rows in all. Rep first through 34th rows 10 more times. With D, bind off.

RIGHT BORDER STRIPS (Make 1A and 1B): A—With D, cast on 10 sts and follow Chart Right A to end of 12th row. Rep first through 12th rows 30 more times; then rep first and 2nd rows once more. With D, bind off. B—With D, cast on 22 sts and follow Chart for Right Border B to end of last row. Rep first through 34th rows 10 more times. With D, bind off.

LEFT BORDER STRIPS (Make 1A and 1B): Following Charts for Left A and Left Border B, work same as for Right Border Strips.

Crochet Edgings: With right side of a Strip 2 facing, using crochet hook, attach A to beg of a long edge of strip. **Row 1:** Sc evenly along side edge of strip to next corner, being careful to keep work flat. Ch 1, turn. **Row 2:** Sc in each sc across. Break off and fasten.

Attach B and ch 1, turn. **Row 3:** With B, work same as last row. Break off and fasten. Attach A and ch 1, turn. **Rows 4-5:** With A, rep Row 2. Break off and fasten. Work edging along opposite side edge of same strip in same way. Work edging along each side edge of other two Strip 2 s in same way. With A, work 2 rows of sc along each side edge of each A Border Strip.

FINISHING: Following Assembling Chart for placement of strips, with A and a darning needle, sew strips together. With right side facing and D, sc evenly along each short edge of afghan. Break off and fasten. Block to measurements. **Fringe:** Wind D several times around a 7" piece of cardboard, cut at one end to make 14" strands. Continue to cut fringe as needed. Hold 2 strands tog and fold in half to form a loop, insert hook from back to front in first sc on one short edge and draw loop through; draw ends through loop and pull tightly to form a knot. Tie two 14" strands in this way in every other sc across short edge. Tie fringe along opposite edge in same way. Trim evenly.

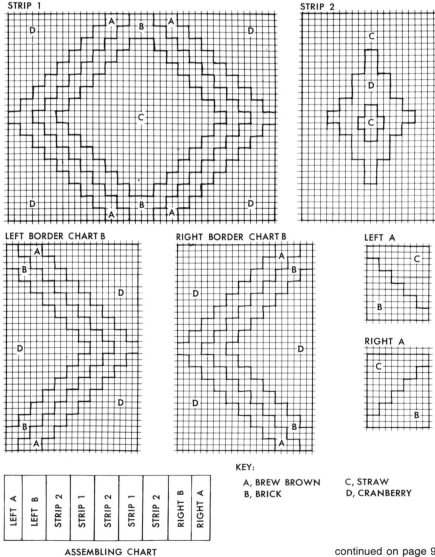

KEY:

A, BREW BROWN   C, STRAW
B, BRICK   D, CRANBERRY

ASSEMBLING CHART

continued on page 98

INDIAN WRAPAROUND

To make afghan see page 95. To **wear** afghan we suggest ¾"-wide elastic to anchor it in place. Take measurement just above bustline to determine the length of elastic and casing (see photo); elastic must be slightly shorter than this measurement for a snug fit to support weight of afghan. Sew flat hook and eye to ends of elastic. Center elastic at wrong side at top of afghan. Pin elastic to top. To form casing, make a slip stitch with leftover wool, above elastic at the right-hand side (see Diagram). Ch 4, make a sl st in second stitch to left in row below elastic. *Ch 4, make sl st four stitches to left above elastic. Ch 4, make sl st four stitches to left below elastic. Rep from * to end of elastic. Slip stitch ends of elastic to afghan. Try on afghan and pin ends of casing together at back; adjust so front fits snugly. Pin back openings closed (the free ends at back will form a tail); sew 25" piece of narrow Velcro® to both sides of back at markings for closing. To hem, fold border to wrong side for desired length; slip stitch with wool.

FOR THE HOME

Enhance your home, for it is the haven that renews your spirit.

Here is patchwork, pure and simple, for an afghan that gets back to the basics . . . a runner that ripples in sunlight and brightens a door . . . quarry tiles in random reds for the rug to warm a room . . . and simple squares placed with sophistication for an afghan that's at home anywhere . . .

DIAMOND AFGHAN

SIZE: Approximately 48" x 56" excluding fringe.

MATERIALS: Brunswick Aspen (2-oz skn): 4 skns #1400 Ecru, 5 skns each of #1412 Royal, #1486 Brew Brown and #1435 Camel. For Fringe (Optional): 2 extra skns of one of above colors. Knitting Needles, 1 pair No. 10½ OR SIZE TO OBTAIN GAUGE. Crochet Hook, Size F.

GAUGE: 3 sts = 1"; 4 rows = 1". Each diamond measures 6" x 8".

NOTE: Afghan is made in strips, then stitched together. Do not break off between diamonds or parts of diamonds until strip is completed.

STRIP A (Make 2 Royal, 4 Camel and 2 Brew Brown—8 strips in all): Cast on one st and p this st. **First Diamond: Row 1:** In st on needle k 1, p 1 and k 1—3 sts. **Row 2:** P across. **Row 3:** Inc in first st, k 1, inc in last st—one st incd at each end. **Row 4:** P across. Continuing in stockinette st (k 1 row; p 1 row), inc one st at each end of every k row until there are 18 sts, ending with p row. Then dec one st at each end of next k row and every k row thereafter until 2 sts rem, ending with p row. K rem 2 sts tog and p this st—diamond completed. Starting with Row 1, continue to work diamonds same as First Diamond until 7 diamonds in all have been completed. Bind off rem st.

STRIP B: (Make 2 Brew Brown, 3 Ecru and 2 Royal Blue—7 strips in all): Cast on 18 sts. **Row 1:** P across. **Row 2:** K across, dec one st at each end. Rep Rows 1-2 until 2 sts rem, ending with p row. **Next row:** K 2 tog—half diamond completed. P rem st. Working same as for First Diamond of Strip A, make 6 complete diamonds; then continue to work as before until there are 18 sts on needle, ending with p row. Bind off.

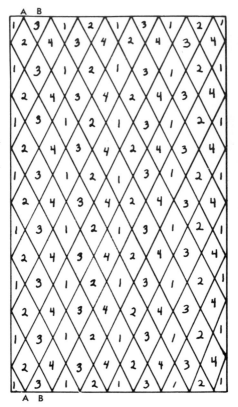

A B

A B

8"

6"

1. ECRU
2. ROYAL BLUE
3. BREW BROWN
4. CAMEL

RIGHT SIDE STRIP: With Ecru, cast on 9 sts. **Row 1:** P across. **Row 2:** K across to within last 2 sts, k 2 tog—dec made at end of row. Rep last 2 rows until 2 sts rem, ending with p row. **Next row:** K 2 tog. **Next row:** P 1—fourth of a diamond completed. **Next row:** K and p in st on needle. **Next row:** P 2. Continuing in stockinette st, inc one st at end of every k row until there are 9 sts, ending with k row. Starting with Row 1, rep directions for Right Side Strip 6 more times. Bind off.

LEFT SIDE STRIP: With Ecru, making decs and incs at beg of every k row (instead of at end of row) thus reversing shaping, work same as for Right Side Strip.

Slip Stitch Trim: With right side facing, insert crochet hook from front to back in first st on a Strip A, using matching color, hold yarn in back of work and draw up lp. Continuing to hold yarn in back of work throughout, crochet loosely one row of sl sts evenly along entire outer edge of first diamond, being careful to adjust tension so that work will not pull. Break off. Work a row of sl sts around each diamond on same strip in same way. Work sl st trim along outer edge of each diamond and each part of a diamond on all strips.

FINISHING: Steam strips lightly through a damp cloth, do not press. Arrange strips as shown on chart; with a large eyed needle and using the color of one of the 2 strips being joined, sew strips together, allowing sl st trim to rem free on right side.

FRINGE (Optional): Using desired color, wind yarn several times around a 6-inch square of cardboard, cut at one edge, thus making 12-inch strands. Continue to cut strands as needed. Hold two 12-inch strands tog and fold in half to form a lp. Insert crochet hook in a st along outer edge of afghan and draw lp through, draw loose ends through lp and pull tight to form knot. Tie groups of two 12-inch strands in same way at 1-inch intervals along entire outer edge.

RIPPLE RUNNER

SIZE: 22" x 40".

MATERIALS: Bernat Berella "4" (2-oz balls), 4 balls Arbutus (A), 9 Biege (B), 8 Ranchero Russet (C). **Note:** Color D is a combination of 1 strand each of B and C.) Knitting Needles, No. 10 OR SIZE TO OBTAIN GUAGE.

GAUGE: Dble strand, 4 sts = 1"; 7 ridges (14 rows—garter st) = 2".

NOTE: Always change colors on wrong side, picking up new color from under dropped color. Use a separate dble strand ball for each color change. Do not carry color across other colors.

NOTE 2: Wind 2 dble strand balls each of color A, 2 dble strand balls each of B and 2 balls each of color D (use 1 strand each B and C).

RUG: Beg at bottom with color A (see Note 2), cast on 14 sts, drop A; with 2nd ball A cast on 14 sts on same needle. Work in garter st (k each row), inc 1 st at each edge of each piece every other row until there are 30 sts on each piece. Work 1 row even; cast on 7 sts at end of 2nd piece. **Next Row:** Mark this row for right side. With A, k 15 sts, drop A; tie in B and k 14 sts, drop B; tie in A and k 8 sts, cast on 14 sts, k 8 sts, drop A; tie in B and k 14 sts; tie in A and k 8 sts; then cast on 7 sts—88 sts. Working color over color, work 1 B st more toward sides on each side of center B sections until there are 30 B sts in each center section. Work 1 row, ending on wrong side. **Next Row:** With B, k 15 sts; with C k 14 sts; with B, k 30 sts; with C, k 14 sts; end with B, k last 15 sts. Working color over color, work 1 C st more toward sides on each side of center C sections until there are 30 B sts in each center section. Work 1 row. Cont in this manner, working following stripes as follows: next color B, D, B, C, A, C, B, D, C, A, B and C; when starting last stripe, bind off first 7 sts, work to within center 30 sts, bind off these 30 sts; k to within last 7 sts and bind off these sts. Working on remaining sts of each piece, dec 1 st each side of each piece every other row until 14 sts remain on each piece. Bind off. Run in ends on wrong side. Block.

QUARRY-TILE RUG

SIZE: Approximately 45″ × 61″.

MATERIALS: American Thread "Aunt Lydia's" Heavy Rug Yarn (70 yd skn). 6 skns Burnt Orange (A), 9 skns Phantom Red (B), 6 skns Brown (C), 5 skns Rust (CR). Knitting Needles, 1 pair No. 7 OR SIZE TO OBTAIN GAUGE. Crochet Hook, Size H.

GAUGE: 4 sts = 1″; 5 rows = 1″.

MEASUREMENTS: Each hexagon measures 3″ on each side; 6″ diagonally from point to point.

STRIPS 1–3–5–7–9: With 1st color indicated on chart cast on 12 sts. **Row 1:** K across row. **Row 2:** P across row. **Row 3:** P 1 and k 1 in 1st st—inc at beg; k across row to within last st, k in front loop of last st, leave on needle, k in back loop of same st, sl st off needle—inc at end. **Row 4:** P across. Rep the Rows 3 and 4 until there are 24 sts on needle. **Next 3 Rows:** P 1 row; k 1 row; p 1 row. **Next Row:** K 1, sl 1 as if to k, psso—dec at beg, k across row to within last 2 sts, k tog—dec at end. **Next Row:** P across row. Rep last 2 rows until there are 12 sts on needle. This completes one hexagon. Following color scheme of chart rep from Row 1 through last row 9 more times. Bind off. **Strips 2–4–6–8:** With 1st color indicated in

chart, cast on 24 sts. **Row 1:** K across row. **Row 2:** P across row. **Row 3:** Dec 1 st at beg and end of row. Rep last 2 rows until there are 12 sts on needle. **Next Row:** P across row—this completes ½ hexagon. Then work 9 hexagons same as for Strip 1 following color scheme on chart. **Next Row:** Change color and work ½ hexagon as follows: Work same as hexagon until there are 24 sts on needle. **Next Row:** P across row. Bind off.

SIDE STRIPS (Make 2): With B, cast on 8 sts. **Row 1:** K across row. **Row 2:** P across row. **Row 3:** K across row, dec 1 st at end of row. Rep last 2 rows until 2 sts remain. **Next 3 Rows:** P 1 row; k 1 row; p 1 row. **Next Row:** K across row, inc at end of row. **Next Row:** P across row. Rep last 2 rows until there are 8 sts on needle. Rep from Row 1 to last row 9 times more. Bind off.

FINISHING: Steam strips lightly. Sew strips tog following chart.

EDGE: With Phantom Red work a row of sc around entire rug, having same number of sc on corresponding sides of rug and 3 sc in each corner st. Join with sl st to first sc. **Next Rnd:** Ch 1, sc in each sc, working 3 sc in each corner st. Join with sl st to first sc. Break off and fasten.

A = ORANGE   **C** = BROWN
B = RED   **CR** = RUST

103

SIZE: Approximately 40″ × 50″.

MATERIALS: Spinnerin Deluxe 4 Ply or Marvel Twist Deluxe Knitting Worsted (4-oz skn): 6 skns Dark Green (DG), 4 skns Medium Green (MG), 2 skns Yellow (Y) and 1 skn Blue (B). Knitting Needles: No. 7 OR SIZE TO OBTAIN GAUGE.

GAUGE: 5 sts = 1″; 7 rows = 1″.

NOTES: 1. Afghan is made up of 32 squares, 14 large triangles (½ square each) and 4 small triangles. 2. DG is **always** worked in garter st (k each row); other colors in stockinette st (k 1 row, p 1 row). 3. One st at beg of every p row (opposite DG edge) should always be knitted to form garter st along edge. 4. When changing colors, pick up color to be used under other color, twisting yarn togs once to prevent making holes in work.

SQUARE (Make 32): With DG, cast on 48 sts. Work 22 rows in garter st (k each row). **Row 23:** K 12 DG; attach MG and k 36 MG. **Row 24:** With MG k 1, p 35; with DG k 12. **Rows 25-38:** Using MG already attached, rep last two rows 7 times. **Row 39:** K 12 DG, 12 MG; attach Y and k 24 Y. **Row 40:** With Y k 1, p 23; p 12 MG; k 12 DG. **Rows 41-54:** Using Y already attached, rep last 2 rows 7 times. **Row 55:** K 12 DG, 12 MG, 12 Y; attach B k 12 B. **Row 56:** With B, k 1, p 11; p 12 Y, 12 MG; k 12 DG. **Rows 57-70:** Using yarns already attached, rep last 2 rows 7 times. Bind off, matching colors.

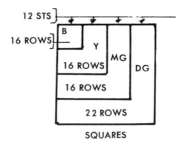

SQUARES

TRIANGLE A (Make 3): With DG, cast on 48 sts. **Rows 1-22:** Working in garter st, dec one st at beg of 2nd row and at beg of every other row thereafter 10 more times—37 sts. **Row 23:** K 12 DG; attach MG and k 25. **Row 24:** With MG, k 1, p 24; k 12 DG. Keeping colors as established and working DG in garter st and MG in stockinette st, * dec one st at **shaped** edge on each of next 3 rows, then work one row even, thus decreasing 3 sts over 4 rows; rep from * until one st rem. Bind off.

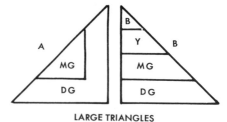

LARGE TRIANGLES

TRIANGLE B (Make 4): With DG, cast on 48 sts. **Rows 1-22:** Work in garter st, dec one st at **end** of 2nd row and at end of every

other row thereafter 10 more times—37 sts. Break off DG. **Next 16 Rows:** With MG, work in stockinette st, * dec one st at **shaped** edge on each of 3 rows, than work 1 row even; rep from * 3 more times—25 sts. Break off MG. **Next 16 rows:** With Y, work same as last sixteen rows—13 sts. **Next 16 rows:** With B, work as last 16 rows—1 st rem. Bind off.

TRIANGLE C (Make 3): With DG, cast on 2 sts. **Rows 1-22:** Work in garter st, inc one st at **end** of 2nd row and every other row thereafter 9 more times—12 sts. Work 2 rows even. Break off DG. **Rows 23-38:** * With MG, k 1 row; then working in stockinette st, inc one st at **shaped** edge on each of next 3 rows thus increasing 3 sts over 4 rows; rep from * 3 more times—24 sts. Drop DG. **Row 39:** With Y, k 24. **Row 40:** K 1, p 23, pick up MG and cast on 2 sts—26 sts. **Row 41:** Using colors as established, k across. **Rows 42-43-44:** Using colors as established, work in stockinette st, inc one st at shaped edge on each row. **Rows 45-54:** Rep last 4 rows twice; then rep Rows 41 and 42 once more—36 sts. **Row 55:** K 12 MG, 12 Y; attach B and k 12. **Row 56:** P 12 B, 12 Y, 12 MG; attach DG and cast on 2 sts—38 sts. **Row 57:** Working colors as established, k across. Continue in pat, increasing at shaped edge as before until there are 12 DG sts. Bind off, matching colors.

TRIANGLE D (Make 4): With DG, cast on 2 sts. **Rows 1-22:** Work in garter st, inc one st at **beg** of 2nd row and every other row thereafter 9 more times—12 sts. Work 2 rows even, ending at straight edge. **Row 23:** Work across row; attach MG and cast on 2 sts. **Row 24:** P 2 MG; complete row. **Rows 25-38:** Working colors as established, work DG in garter st and all other sts in stockinette st, * inc one st at **shaped** edge on each of 3 rows, than work 1 row even; rep from * until there are 12 MG sts. Work 1 row even, ending at straight edge—24 sts. **Row 39:** Matching colors, K across; attach Y and cast on 2 sts. With Y instead of MG, rep Rows 24-38. There are 36 sts. **Next Row:** Matching colors, k across; attach B and cast on 2 sts. With B instead of MG, rep Rows 24-38. There are 48 sts. Bind off, matching colors.

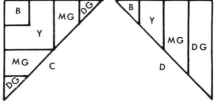

LARGE TRIANGLES

TRIANGLE E: With DG, cast on 2 sts. Inc one st at **beg** of 2nd row and every other row thereafter 4 more times—7 sts. K next row; attach MG and cast on 2 sts. Work 1 row even. (Inc 3 sts over 4 rows as before) along shaped edge) twice—15 sts. Dec sts to correspond with inc sts until 2 sts rem. Bind off.

TRIANGLE F: With DG, cast on 24 sts. Dec one st each end of 2nd row and every other row 4 more times—14 sts. Break off DG. Attach MG and working in stockinette st, * dec one at each end of 3 rows, then work 1 row even; rep from * until 2 sts rem. Bind off.

TRIANGLE G: With DG, cast on 2 sts. Inc one st at **end** of 2nd row and every other row 4 more times, ending with an inc row—7 sts. Break off DG. Attach MG. Working in stockinette st, (inc one st at shaped edge on each of 3 rows, then work 1 row even) twice—13 sts. Break off MG. Attach Y and (dec one st at shaped edge on each of 3 rows, work 1 row even) twice. Break off Y. Attach B and continue decs as for Y until 2 sts rem. Bind off.

TRIANGLE H: With MG, cast on one st; with Y, cast on one st on same needle. **Row 1:** Matching colors, k, cast on 2 sts at end of row. **Row 2:** Matching colors, p across, cast on 2 sts. **Row 3:** K across. **Row 4:** Matching colors, p across, cast on 2 sts. **Rows 5-8:** Rep last 4 rows—14 sts. **Row 9:** Always working sts as established, k across; attach B and cast on 2 sts. **Row 10:** P across; attach DG and cast on 2 sts. **Row 11:** K across. Work in stockinette st, inc one st at each end of next 3 rows, then work 1 row even. Inc one st at each end of next row; work 1 row even. Bind off, matching colors.

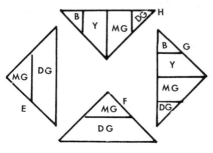

SMALL TRIANGLES

FINISHING: Steam pieces lightly through a damp cloth. Following Afghan Chart, sew squares and triangles tog. **Border: Rnd 1:** With right side facing and matching colors, sc evenly along entire outer edge, being careful to keep work flat and making 3 sc in same st at each corner. Join with sl st to first sc. **Rnd 2:** Ch 1, sc in same sc used for joining, matching colors, sc in each sc, making 3 sc in center sc of each 3-sc group. Join. Break off and fasten. Steam Border.

AFGHAN CHART

FOR CHILDREN

Decide on a gift the way a child does: pick the colors that make you happy and begin. [Have fun and (any child will tell you) it will be as perfect as it can be.]

Here's a scarf with a cheerful sense of color that a child can knit for her best friend. And here are sweaters just the way children like them: one striped just right for blue jeans . . . two that are miniature editions of Fair Isle classics . . . a cable stitch tennis sweater for a boy— and his teddy bear . . . and even a sweater spotted like a puppy (why not make a sweater to make a child laugh?). Here are socks, mittens and caps that grow to grown-up size . . . and a lion in summer, basking in sunshine.

SIZES: Directions are for size 3. Changes for sizes 4 and 6 are in parentheses.

MATERIALS: Reynolds Gleneagles (50 g r balls) 5-(6-7) balls Red (A), 1 ball each of Black (B) and White (C); 6 (8-8") zipper; ¾ yard ½" wide elastic. Knitting Needles, 1 pair each No. 1 and No. 3 OR SIZE TO OBTAIN GAUGE.

GAUGE: 7½ sts = 1"; 10 rows = 1".

BLOCKING MEASUREMENTS: Dress: Chest—24 (26-28)"; width of back or front at underarms—12 (13-14)"; width of sleeve at upperarm—7 (8-9)". Bloomers: Waist—21 (22-23)"; width of front or back—14 (15-16)".

DRESS: FRONT: With No. 1 needles and A cast on 88 (98-108) sts. Work in stockinette st (k 1 row, p 1 row) for 9 rows, inc 1 st each end of every k row—98 (108-118) sts. **Next Row:** (wrong side): K for hemline. Change to No. 3 needles. **Row 1:** Inc in first st, k to last st, inc in last st. **Row 2:** P. **Row 3:** Repeat row 1. **Row 4:** P 1, keeping yarn in front sl 1 as if to p, p to last 2 sts, keeping yarn in front sl 1 as if to p, p 1. **Row 5:** Repeat row 1. **Row 6:** P 2, keeping yarn in front sl 1 as if to p, p to last 3 sts keeping yarn in front sl 1 as if to p, p 2. Continue to inc 1 st at each end of right side rows and keeping sl st correct on wrong side rows. Complete 10 rows above hemline —108 (118-128) sts. Keeping 5th st at each end as a sl st on wrong side rows, continue to work even until 26 rows above hemline have been completed, ending on wrong side. Bind off 5 sts at beg·of next 2 rows—98 (108-118) sts. Work even for 2 rows. Continue in stockinette st, dec 1 st at each end of next row, then every 12th row 3 (4-5) times more—90 (98-106) sts. Work even until piece measures 7 (8½-11)" above hemline, ending on wrong side. Join C and work even for 8 rows. Join B and work even for 4 rows. Break off B. With C work even for 8 rows. Break off C. Continue with A until piece measures 10 (11½-14)" above hemline. Mark last row.

ARMHOLES: Bind off 3 sts at beg of next 2 rows. Dec 1 st at each end of next 6 (6-7) rows; then every other row 2 (3-3) times—68 (74-80) sts. Work even until armholes measures 3 (3½-4)" above marked row, ending on wrong side.

NECK: Next Row: K 22 (24-26) sts; turn, leaving remaining sts on spare needle.

Continue on first set of sts as follows: **Row 1:** P 1, p 2 tog, p to end. **Row 2:** K. Repeat last 2 rows 4 times more—17 (19-21) sts, ending with row 1.

SHOULDERS: Bind off 5 (6-7) sts at armhole edge every other row twice, then 7 sts once. Return to spare needle, sl 24 (26-28) sts onto holder for front neck. Join yarn to remaining sts. **Row 1:** K 1, sl 1, k 1, psso, k to end. **Row 2:** P. Repeat last 2 rows 4 times more—17 (19-21) sts, ending with row 1. Shape shoulder as for first set of sts.

BACK: Work same as front until piece measures 9 (9-12)" above hemline, ending on wrong side. **Divide for Back Opening: Next Row:** K 45 (49-53) sts; turn, leaving remaining sts on spare needle. Work even on first set of sts until piece measures same as front to armhole, ending on wrong side.

ARMHOLE: Bind off 3 sts at beg of next row. Work 1 row. Dec 1 st at armhole edge on next 6 (6-7) rows, then every other row 2 (3-3) times—34 (37-40) sts. Work even until armhole measures same as front to shoulder, ending at armhole edge.

SHOULDER: Bind off 5 (6-7) sts at armhole edge every other row twice, then 7 sts once—17 (18-19) sts. Sl remaining sts onto holder for back neck. Join yarn to inner edge of 45 (49-53) sts and complete to correspond with first set of sts.

SLEEVES: With No. 1 needles and A cast on 44 (48-52) sts. Work in stockinette st for 9 rows. **Next Row** (wrong side): K for hemline. Change to No. 3 needles. Beg with a k row, continue in stockinette st inc 1 st each end of 11th row, then every 8th row 3 (5-7) times—52 (60-68) sts. Work even until sleeve length is 6 (7-8)" above hemline.

TOP SHAPING: Bind off 3 sts at beg of next 2 rows. Dec 1 st at beg of next 10 rows. Bind off 2 sts at beg of next 8 (10-12) rows. Bind off remaining sts.

NECKBAND: Sew shoulder seams. Using No. 1 needles and A, with right side facing you, beg at left back neck, pick up and k 74 (78-82) sts around neck including sts on holders. Beg with a p row, work in stockinette st for 6 rows. **Next Row** (wrong side): K for hemline. Beg with a k row, work in stockinette st for 5 rows. Bind off.

BLOOMERS: FRONT: With No. 1 needles and A cast on 35 (38-41) sts for

right leg. Work in stockinette st for 7 rows. **Next Row:** (wrong side): K for hemline. Beg with a k row, work in stockinette st for 7 rows. **Next Row:** P 2, * (inc 1 st in next st, p 2). Repeat from * to end—46 (50-54) sts. Change to No. 3 needles. Join C. Beg with a k row, work in stockinette st for 4 rows C, 2 rows B, 4 rows C. Break off B and C. Work 2 rows A. Leave these sts on spare needle. Work another piece in same manner for left front leg.

JOINING: Row 1 (right side): K across sts of left leg; turn, cast on 12 sts for crotch, then k across sts for right leg—104 (112-120) sts. **Row 2 and all even rows:** P. **Row 3:** K 45 (49-53); k 2 tog through back loop, k 10, k 2 tog; k 45 (49-53) sts—102 (110-118) sts. **Row 5:** K 45 (49-53); k 2 tog through back loop, k 8, k 2 tog; k 45 (49-53) sts—100 (108-116) sts. Continue to dec 2 sts as above on every right side row until 92 (100-108) sts remain. Work even until piece measures 3 (4-5)" from cast-on sts of crotch, ending on wrong side (adjust length here if required). Dec 1 st at each end of next row, then every 6th row 3 times—84 (92-100) sts. P 1 row. Change to No. 1 needles and work in k 1, p 1 ribbing for 1". Bind off in ribbing.

BACK: Work as for front until back is 1 row less than front to waist rib, ending on right side. **Next Row:** P 76 (80-84); turn. **Next Row:** K 68; turn. **Next Row:** P 56; turn. **Next Row:** K 44; turn. **Next Row:** P 32; turn. **Next Row:** K 20; turn. **Next Row:** P to end. Change to No. 1 needles and work in k 1, p 1 ribbing for 1". Bind off in ribbing.

FINISHING: Block pieces to measurements. Sew in sleeves. Join sleeve seams and side seams to top of side openings. Turn in facings to sl st at sides and hem down. Turn up hems at lower edge, sleeves and neckband and sew on wrong side. Sew in zipper. Join side and inner leg seams of bloomers. Turn up hems at lower edge. Make herringbone casing (see diagram) at waist, thread elastic through and secure. Press all seams.

TEDDY'S STRIPED SCARF

SIZE: 10½" wide by 52" long.

NOTE: Scarf may be knit to any length, and width may be changed by adding or subtracting cast-on stitches.

MATERIALS: 4-ply knitting worsted in 10 to 12 assorted colors of your choice. Knitting needles, 1 pair No. 10 OR SIZE TO OBTAIN GAUGE.

GAUGE: 7 sts = 2"; 7 rows = 1".

TO MAKE: Cast on 42 stitches. Make a striped border of 10 or 11 different colors, working 5 to 7 rows of each color. See Basic Knitting, page 13 for how to change colors.

Work alternate stripes of garter stitch (knit each row) and stockinette stitch (knit 1 row, purl 1 row) or mix garter and stockinette stitch patterns within one color stripe. Picking any one of stripe colors for center of scarf, work that color in stockinette stitch for about 30" or desired length. Repeat border, working colors in reverse order. Bind off.

CHILD'S AND DOLL'S STRIPED SWEATERS

SIZES: Directions are for size 2. Changes for sizes 3 and 4 are in parentheses.

MATERIALS: Bear Brand, Fleisher's or Botany Machine Washable Spectator (2 oz balls): 1 (2-2) balls each of colors A and B. Knitting Needles, 1 pair each of Nos. 3 and 5 OR SIZE TO OBTAIN GAUGE. Crochet Hook, No. 0 (zero). 3 small buttons.

GAUGE: On No. 5 needles—6 sts = 1"; 8 rows = 1".

BLOCKING MEASUREMENTS: Chest —22 (23-24)". Width of back or front at underarm—11 (11½-12)". Width of sleeve at upper arm—7 (7½-8)".

CHILD'S SWEATER — BACK: With A and No. 3 needles, cast on 65 (69-73) sts. **Ribbing: Row 1 (wrong side):** P 1, *k 1, p 1; rep from * across. **Row 2:** K 1, *p 1, k 1; rep from * across. Rep Rows 1 and 2 until there are 15 rows in all, end with wrong-side row. Drop A. Attach B; change to No. 5 needles. Work in stripe pat as follows: **Rows 1-2:** With B, work in st st (k 1 row, p 1 row). Drop B, pick up A. **Rows 3-4:** With A, work in st st. Drop A; pick up B. Rep last 4 rows for stripe pat. Work in pat until 7 (7½-8)" from beg, end with a p row.

ARMHOLES: Continuing in pat throughout, bind off 3 sts at beg of next 2 rows. **Next Row:** K 1, sl 1, k 1, psso, k across to within last 3 sts, k 2 tog, k 1—one st decreased at each end. Continuing in pat, dec one st at each end same as before every other row 1 (2-2) more times—55 (57-61) sts. Work even in pat until 4 (4¼-4½)" from first row of armholes.

SHOULDERS: Bind off 8 sts at beg of next 2 rows, then 8 (8-9) sts at beg of following 2 rows—23 (25-27) sts.

Neckband: Change to No. 3 needles and with A, k 1 row. Rep ribbing Rows 1-2 for 7 rows in all. Bind off loosely in ribbing.

FRONT: Work same as for Back until 2¾" from first row of armholes, end with right-side row of a B stripe.

NECK: P 20 (20-21) and place these sts just worked on a stitch holder; p next 15 (17-19) sts and place these sts on another stitch holder to be used for neckband; p rem 20 (20-21) sts. Working over sts on needle only, k 1 row. Working in pat, bind off 2 sts at neck edge at beg of next row and at beg of following p row once more— 16 (16-17) sts. Work even until armhole is same length as on Back, end at armhole edge.

SHOULDER: Bind off 8 sts at beg of next row. Work 1 row even. Bind off rem 8 (8-9) sts. Slip the 20 (20-21) sts from first holder onto a No. 5 needle, attach yarn at neck edge and complete to correspond with opposite side, reversing shaping.

Neckband: With right side facing, using A and No. 3 needles, pick up and k 7 (8-9) sts along left front neck edge, k 15 (17-19) sts on holder, pick up and k 7 (8-9) sts along right front neck edge —29 (33-37) sts. Work in ribbing as for Back for 7 rows. Bind off loosely in ribbing.

SLEEVES: With A and No. 3 needles, cast on 41 (43-45) sts. Work in ribbing same as for Back for 7 rows, end with

a wrong-side row. Change to No. 5 needles. Work in stripe pat same as for Back until 2 (2½-3)" from beg, ending with same pat row as on Back to underarm.

Top Shaping: Continuing in pat, bind off 3 sts at beg of next 2 rows. Dec one st at each end every other row 7 (8-9) times in all. Bind off 2 sts at beg of next 4 rows. Bind off rem 13 sts.

FINISHING: Block pieces to measurements. Sew side, sleeve and right shoulder seams. Starting at armhole edge, sew about ¾" seam at left shoulder.

Edging: With right side facing and using crochet hook, attach A with sl st to first free st (after seam) on left front shoulder edge, sc evenly along front edge to end of neckband. Break off and fasten. With right side facing, attach A with sl st at end of neckband on back edge of left shoulder, sc evenly across to seam. Ch 1, turn. **Next Row:** With pins, mark the position of 3 button loops evenly spaced along last row; *sc in each sc to within next pin, ch 2, sk next sc for button loop; rep from * 2 more times; sc in each rem sc. Break off and fasten. Sew on buttons on opposite edge.

DOLL'S SWEATER—BACK: With A and No. 5 needles, cast on 38 sts. Work in stripe pat same as for Child's Sweater for 4½" from beg.

SHOULDERS: Continuing in pat, bind off 2 sts at beg of next 8 rows. Bind off.

FRONT: Work same as for Back. Sew shoulder seams. Sew side seams for 2½" from lower edge.

SIZES: Directions are for size 4. Changes for 6 and 8 in parentheses.

MATERIALS: Brunswick Pomfret Sport (2 oz skn): #528 Fawn Heather (MC) — 3 (4-5) skns. 1 skn each of #511 Schooner Blue, #5101 Strato Blue, #512 Royal Blue, #503 Lt. Yellow, #531 Maize, #5000 Cream and #557 Cranberry. Knitting Needles: 1 pr each No. 3 and No. 5 or SIZE TO OBTAIN GAUGE. 8 buttons.

GAUGE: 6 sts = 1"; 7 rows = 1".

Note: Cardigan is worked in one piece to underarms.

BODY: With No. 3 needles and MC cast on 145 (157-169) sts. **Ribbing—Row 1:** K 1, * p 1, k 1; rep from * across. **Row 2:** P 1, * k 1, p 1; rep from* across. Rep these 2 rows for 2½". Change to No. 5 needles. K 1 row, p 1 row. Read chart from right to left on k rows and from left to right on p rows. Rep the 12 sts of the chart across, ending as shown. Carry color not in use loosely on wrong side of work. Cut off colors when no longer needed. Complete the 15 rows of chart and continue with MC in st st until 9½ (11-12)" from beg or desired length to underarms, end with a p row. **Dividing Row:** K 29 (32-35), bind off next 12 sts, work until 63 (69-75) sts from bind off, bind off next 12 sts, finish row.

LEFT FRONT: At armhole edge dec 1 st every other row 4 times—25 (28-31) sts. Work even until 2½ (2¾-4)" above underarm, ending at front edge.

Neck and Shoulder: Bind off 12 (13-14) sts at beg of next row. **Dec. Row:** K to within 3 sts of neck edge, k 2 tog, k 1. Rep dec every other row 4 times more—8 (10-12) sts. Work even until 4¾ (5¼-5¾)" above underarm. From armhole edge bind off all sts.

RIGHT FRONT: Work to correspond to left front, reversing all shaping. Work neck decs as follows: K 1, sl 1, k 1, psso, k to end of row.

BACK: Dec 1 st each side every other row 5 times—53 (59-65) sts. Work even until 3 (3¼-3½)" above underarms, end with a p row.

NECK AND SHOULDERS: K 12 (14-16) sts, place next 29 (31-33) sts on a holder, join another ball of yarn, finish row. Dec 1 st at each side of neck, same as fronts, every other row 4 times—8 (10-12) sts each side. Work even until armhole measures same as fronts. From armhole edges bind off all sts.

SLEEVES: With No. 3 needles and MC cast on 43 (45-47) sts. K 1, p 1 in ribbing for 3" and inc 6 (4-2) sts evenly spaced on last row —49 sts. Change to No. 5 needles. K 1 row, p 1 row. Follow chart as on body for fifteen rows. Continue with MC only in st st and inc 1 st each side every 6th row 3 (4-5) times—55 (57-59) sts. Work even until sleeve measures 12½ (13-14)" or desired length.

Shaping: Bind off 6 sts at beg of next 2 rows. Dec 1 st each side every other row 7 (8-9) times. Bind off 3 sts at beg of next 6 rows. Bind off rem sts. Sew shoulder seams.

NECKBAND: With No. 5 needles and MC pick up and k 97 (97-109) sts all around neck edge including sts on holders. P 1 row. Work 15 rows of chart as lower edge. Change to No. 3 needles, p 1 row and dec 20 (16-24) sts evenly spaced. Work in ribbing on 77 (81-85) sts for 1¼". Bind off in ribbing.

FRONT BORDERS: Make border without buttonholes first; right front for boys, left front for girls. With No. 3 needles and MC cast on 9 sts. Work in ribbing until band reaches from lower edge to neck. Bind off. Mark position for 8 buttons on border sts with top and lowest markers ½" from edges, space others evenly between. **Buttonhole Border:** Work as first band to marker. **Buttonholes:** Work 3 sts, bind off next 2 sts, work to end. Next row cast on 2 sts over the bound off sts.

FINISHING: Sew side and sleeve seams. Sew in sleeves. Sew front border sts in place. Sew on buttons.

CHILD'S FAIR ISLE PULLOVER

SIZES: Directions are for size 4. Changes for 6 and 8 in parentheses.

MATERIALS: Brunswick Pomfret Sport (2 oz skn): #528 Fawn Heather (MC) — 3 (4-5) skns; 1 skn each of #511 Schooner Blue, #5101 Strato Blue, #512 Royal Blue, #503 Lt. Yellow, #5000 Cream, #557 Cranberry. Knitting Needles: 24" Circular needles No. 3 and No. 5 OR SIZE TO OBTAIN GAUGE. One set of No. 3 and No. 5 dp needles for neckband.

GAUGE: 6 sts = 1"; 7 rows = 1".

Note: Pullover is worked in one piece to underarms.

BODY: With No. 3 circular needle and MC, cast on 144 (156-168) sts. Join being careful not to twist sts. Mark beg of rnds. K 1, p 1 in ribbing for 2½". Change to No. 5 needles. K 2 rnds. Rep the 12 sts of chart through row 15. Carry color not in use loosely on wrong side of work. Continue with MC in st st (k every rnd) until 9½ (11-12½)" from beg or desired length to underarms. End at beg of rnd. **Dividing Rnd:** K 66 (72-78) sts, bind off next 12 sts, k to within 6 sts at end of rnd, bind off next 12 sts. Place 60 (66-72) sts of back on a holder.

FRONT: Work back and forth in st st (k 1 row, p 1 row). Dec 1 st each end of every other row 4 times—52 (58-64) sts. Work even until 2½ (2⅔-3)" above underarms, end with a p row.

NECK AND SHOULDERS: K 13 (15-17) sts, place next 26 (28-30) sts on a holder, join another ball of yarn, finish row. Working on sts of both sides dec 1 st each side of neck every other row 5 times as follows: K to within 3 sts of neck edge, k 2 tog, k 1; on other side k 1, sl 1, k 1, psso, k to end—8 (10-12) sts each side. Work even until 4¾ (5¼-5¾)" above underarms. From each armhole edge bind off all sts.

BACK: Work same as front until 3 (3¼-3½)" above underarms. End with a p row.

NECK AND SHOULDERS: K 12 (14-16) sts, place next 28 (30-32) sts on a holder, join another ball of yarn, finish row. Dec 1 st each side of neck in same manner as front every other row 4 times—8 (10-12) sts. Work even until armhole measures same as back. At each armhole edge, bind off all sts.

SLEEVES: With No. 3 needles and MC, cast on 42 (44-46) sts. Work back and forth in k 1, p 1 ribbing for 3" and inc 6 (4-2) sts evenly spaced on last row. Change to No. 5 needles—48 sts. K 1 row, p 1 row. **Note:** Read chart from right to left on k rows and from left to right on p rows. Cut off colors at end of rows when no longer needed. When 15 rows of chart have been completed continue with MC only in st st and inc 1 st each every 6th row 3 (4-5) times—54 (56-58) sts. Work even until sleeve measures 12½ (13-14)" or desired length.

SHAPING: Bind off 6 sts at beg of next 2 rows. Dec 1 st each side every other row 7 (8-9) times. Bind off 3 sts at beg of next 6 rows. Bind off rem sts.

Sew shoulder seams.

NECKBAND: With No. 5 dp needles and MC, pick up and k 96 (96-108) sts all around neck edge including sts on holders. K 1 rnd. Work the 15 rows of chart. Change to No. 3 dp needles. K 1 rnd and dec 20 (16-24) sts evenly spaced — 76 (80-84) sts K 1, p 1 in ribbing for 1". Bind off loosely in ribbing.

FINISHING: Sew sleeve seams. Sew sleeves in place.

FAIR ISLE PULLOVER CHART   **FAIR ISLE CARDIGAN CHART**

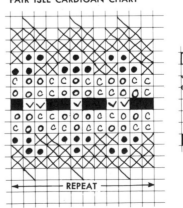

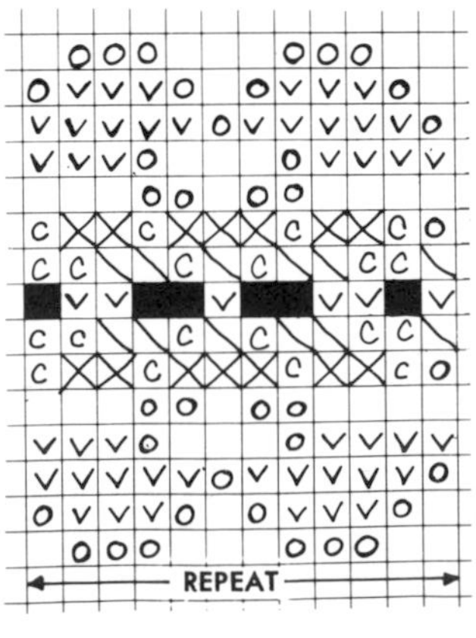

	FAWN HEATHER (MC)
O	SCHOONER BLUE
O	STRATO BLUE
╲	ROYAL BLUE
C	LT. YELLOW
●	MAIZE
V	CREAM
■	CRANBERRY

SIZES: Directions are for Boy's size 4. Changes for sizes 6, 8 and 10 are in parentheses.

MATERIALS: Coats and Clark's "Red Heart" Knitting Worsted, 4 ply (4 oz skn): 9 (10-11-12) ozs of #1 White (W) and 1 oz each of #858 Navy (N) and #903 Devil Red (R). Knitting Needles, 1 pair each Nos. 5 and 7 OR SIZE TO OBTAIN GAUGE. 1 Dp Needle, No. 7.5 small buttons for Teddy Bear's sweater.

GAUGE: Stockinette st—5 sts=1"; 7 rows =1". Cable panel=1".

BLOCKING MEASUREMENTS: Chest—24 (25-27-29)". Width of back or front at underarm—12 (12½-13½-14½)". Width of sleeve at upper arm—9½ (10½-11-11½)".

Note: Teddy Bear's Sweater buttons all the way down the center back.

BOY'S SWEATER—BACK: Start at lower edge with W and No.5 needles, cast on 69 (71-77-83) sts. **Row 1 (right side):** K 1, * p 1, k 1; rep from * across. **Row 2:** P 1, * k 1, p 1; rep from * across; rep Rows 1-2 alternately for 2", end with a wrong-side row and inc one st on last row—70 (72-78-84) sts. Change to No. 7 needles and work in pat as follows: **Row 1:** K 14 (14-15-16), * p 1, k 6, p 1, k 9 (10-12-14); rep from * once; p 1, k 6, p 1, k 14 (14-15-16). **Row 2:** P 14 (14-15-16), * k 1, p 6, k 1, p 9 (10-12-14); rep from * once; k 1, p 6, k 1, p 14 (14-15-16). **Row 3:** K 14 (14-15-16), * p 1, **slip next 3 sts onto a dp needle and hold in front of work, k next 3 sts, k the 3 sts from dp needle—cable twist made;** p 1, k 9 (10-12-14); rep from * once; p 1, cable twist over next 6 sts, p 1, k 14 (14-15-16). **Row 4:** Rep Row 2. **Rows 5-10:** Rep Rows 1-2 alternately 3 times. Rep last 8 rows (Rows 3-10) for pat until total length is 9 (10-11-11½)", end with a wrong-side row.

ARMHOLES: Keeping continuity of pat throughout, bind off 4 (4-5-6) sts at beg of next 2 rows. Dec one st at each end every other row 4 (4-5-6) times—54 (56-58-60) sts. Work even in pat until length is 5 (5½-6-6¼)" from beg of armholes, end with a wrong-side row.

SHOULDERS: Row 1: Keeping continuity of pat, bind off 5 (6-6-7) sts at beg of next 4 rows. Bind off 6 (5-5-4) sts at beg of following 2 rows. Place rem 22 (22-24-24) sts on a st holder for back of neck.

FRONT: Work same as Back until total length is 9 (10-11-11½)", end with a wrong side row.

ARMHOLES: Keeping continuity of pat, bind off 4 (4-5-6) sts at beg of next 2 rows. Dec one st at each end of next row. Work one row even.

NECK: Row 1: Keeping continuity of pat, dec one st at beg of row, work across until there are 26 (27-29-31) sts on right-hand needle, k 2 tog. Place rem 31 (32-34-36) sts on a stitch holder. **Row 2:** Working over sts on needle only, work in pat across. **Row 3:** Dec one st at each end, work in pat across. **Row 4:** Work in pat across. Rep last 2 rows

1 (1-2-3) more times. Keeping armhole edge straight, dec one st at neck edge on next row and every 4th (4th-5th-5th) row thereafter until 16 (17-17-18) sts rem. If necessary work even in pat until length of armhole is same as on Back, end at armhole edge.

SHOULDER: Row 1: Bind off 5 (6-6-7) sts; complete row. **Row 2:** Work in pat across. Rep last 2 rows once. Bind off. Leave center 2 sts on front holder, slip 29 (30-32-34) sts onto a No. 7 needle; attach yarn at neck edge and work to correspond with opposite side, reversing shaping.

SLEEVES: Start at lower edge with W and No. 5 needles, cast on 33 (39-41-43) sts. Work ribbing same as for Back for 2", end with a wrong-side row and inc 7 sts evenly spaced on last row—40 (46-48-50) sts. Change to No. 7 needles and work pat as follows: **Row 1:** K 16 (19-20-21), p 1, k 6, p 1, k 16 (19-20-21). **Row 2:** P 16 (19-20-21), k 1, p 6, k 1, p 16 (19-20-21). Drop W, attach N. **Row 3:** With N, k 16 (19-20-21), p 1, cable twist over next 6 sts same as on Back, p 1, k 16 (19-20-21). **Row 4:** P 16 (19-20-21), k 1, p 6, k 1, p 16 (19-20-21). Break off N; pick up W. **Rows 5-6:** With W, rep Rows 1-2. Drop W; attach R. **Rows 7-8:** With R, rep Rows 1-2. Break off R. **Rows 9-10:** With W, rep Rows 1-2. **With W only,** work same as for Rows 3-10 for pat. Work even in pat until total length is 4", end with a wrong-side row. Keeping continuity of cable panel, inc one st at each end of next row and every 8 (10-10-12) rows thereafter until there are 50 (56-58-60) sts. Work even until total length is 10½ (11½-13-14)", end with a wrong-side row.

Top Shaping: Continuing in pat, bind off 4 (4-5-6) sts at beg of next 2 rows. Dec one st at each and every other row until 22 (26-24-22) sts rem. Bind off 3 (4-3-3) sts at beg of next 4 rows. Bind off rem 10 (10-12-10) sts.

FINISHING: Block pieces to measurements. Sew right shoulder seam. **Neckband:** Right side facing, with W and No. 5 needles, pick up and k 31 (33-35-37) sts along left front neck edge, k one st from front holder, place a marker on needle, k the 2nd st from holder, pick up and k 32 (34-36-38) sts along right front neck edge, k the 22 (22-24-24) sts on back holder—87 (91-97-101) sts. Drop W; attach N. **Row 1:** With N, p across to within 2 sts before next marker, p 2 tog, sl marker, p 2 tog, p to end. **Row 2:** P 1, * k 1, p 1; rep from * across to within 2 sts before marker, k 2 tog, slip marker, sl 1, k 1, psso, p 1, complete row in k 1, p 1 ribbing. Break off N. **Row 3:** With W, work same as Row 1. **Row 4:** With W, work in ribbing as established across to within 2 sts before marker, k 2 tog, sl marker, sl 1, k 1, psso; complete row in ribbing as established. **Rows 5-6:** With R, rep Rows 1 and 4. Break off R. **Row 7:** With W, rep Row 1. Bind off in ribbing, decreasing one st at each side of marker as before. Sew left shoulder and neckband seam. Sew side and sleeve seams. Sew in sleeves.

TEDDY BEAR'S SWEATER: Start at lower edge with W and No. 7 needles, cast on 57

sts. **Row 1 (right side):** K 3 for button band, p 1, * k 1, p 1; rep from * across to within last 3 sts, k 3 for buttonhole band. **Row 2:** K 4, p 1, * k 1, p 1; rep from * across to within last 4 sts, k 4. **Rows 3-4:** Rep Rows 1-2, inc one st at center on last row—58 sts. **Note: First and last 3 sts are worked in garter st (k each row) throughout.** Now work pat as follows. **Row 1:** K 25, p 1, k 6, p 1, k 25. **Row 2:** K 3, p 22, k 1, p 6, k 1, p 22, k 3. **Row 3:** K 25, p 1, twist cable over next 6 sts same as on Boy's Sweater, p 1, k 25. **Rows 4-10:** Rep Rows 2-1 alternately 3 times; then rep Row 2 once more. Last 8 rows (Rows 3-10) form pat. Work in pat until there are 20 rows above ribbing, end with a wrong-side row.

ARMHOLES: K across first 10 sts for Left Back, place rem 48 sts on a st holder. Working over sts on needle only, continue to work buttonband in garter st and all other sts in st st until there are 14 rows on armholes, end with a wrong-side row.

NECK and SHOULDER: Row 1: Bind off 3 sts; complete row. Dec one st at neck edge on each of next 3 rows. Bind off. Leave center 38 sts on holder, sl rem 10 sts onto a No. 7 needle and work Right Back to correspond with opposite side.

FRONT: Place the 38 sts from holder on a No. 7 needle, continuing cable panel, bind off 6 sts at beg of next 2 rows for underarm—26 sts.

NECK: Work across 11 sts, k 2 tog, place rem 13 sts on a st holder. Work in st st over sts on needle only, dec one st at neck edge on next row and every other row thereafter 8 times in all. Work 2 rows even. Bind off rem 4 sts. Sl the 13 sts from holder onto a No. 7 needle, attach yarn at center front, and work to correspond with opposite side.

SLEEVES: Start at lower edge with No. 7 needles and W, cast on 18 sts. Work in k 1, p 1 ribbing for 4 rows. Now work as follows: **Row 1:** K 5, p 1, twist cable over next 6 sts, p 1, k 5. Break off W; attach N. **Row 2:** With N, p 5, k 1, p 6, k 1, p 5. Break off N. **Row 3:** Attach W and work same as Row 1. Break off W. **Row 4:** With R, work same as Row 2. Break off R. With W only, continue in pat as established, twisting cable every 8th row as before until there are 16 rows above ribbing, end with a wrong-side row. **Top Shaping:** Keeping continuity of pat, bind off 3 sts at beg of next 2 rows. Dec one st at each end every other row until 4 sts rem. Bind off.

FINISHING: Block. Sew shoulder, side and sleeve seams. Sew in sleeves. **Neckband:** Right side facing, with W and No. 5 needles, attach yarn to first st of left back neck edge, pick up and k 24 sts along left back and left front of neck to center front; place a marker on needle, pick up and k 24 sts along right front and right back neck edge—48 sts. **Row 1:** With N, p across to within 2 sts before marker, p 2 tog, slip marker, p 2 tog, p to end. **Row 2:** With W, k to within 2 sts before marker, k 2 tog, slip marker, k 2 tog, k across. **Row 3:** With R, rep Row 1. With W, bind off as if to k, decreasing at center front as before. Sew on buttons evenly spaced along left back band. Push buttons between sts on opposite band to fasten.

SIZES: Directions are for Size 2. Changes for Sizes 4 and 6 are in parentheses.

MATERIALS: Dawn Odyssey, 4 oz pull skein —2 (2, 3) White (A), 1 Brown (B). Small amount of Red (C) for neckband. Knitting needles Nos. 6 and 8 OR SIZE TO OBTAIN GAUGE. Small piece of yellow felt.

GAUGE: No. 8 needle: 5 sts = 1".

NOTE: Twist yarns on wrong side when changing colors to prevent holes.

SWEATER

BACK: With No. 6 needles and A, cast on 54 (58, 62) sts. Work in k 2, p 2 ribbing for 1¼". Change to No. 8 needle and stock. st. Work even 1½" above border, ending with a p row. **BACK PATCH: Row 1:** K 49 (53, 57) A, attach B, k 5 B. **Row 2:** P 5 B, p 49 (53, 57) A. **Row 3:** k 48 (52, 56) A, k 6 B. **Row 4:** P 6 B, p 48 (52, 56) A. Continue to work in this manner, working 1 st more in B and 1 st less in A on every other row 15 times more. Work even in colors as established for 14 rows, then work 1 st less in B and 1 st more in A every other row until there are 5 B sts. Remainder of Back worked with A. **AT THE SAME TIME,** when 7 (7½, 8)" from beg, or desired length to underarm, **SHAPE ARM-HOLES:** Bind off 4 sts beg next 2 rows. Dec 1 st each end every other row 3 times — 40 (44, 48) sts. Work even until armhole measures 4½ (5, 5½)". **SHAPE SHOULDERS:** Bind off 5 sts beg next 2 rows, 4 (5, 6) sts beg next 2 rows — 22 (24, 26) sts. Place remaining sts on a holder.

FRONT: Work same as Back for lower border. Change to No. 8 needle and stock. st. Work even until 5" from beg (this includes border), ending with a p row. **LEFT SIDE PATCH:** Row 1: K 8 B, k 46 (50, 54) A. Row 2: P 46 (50, 54) A, p 8 B. Row 3: K 9 B, k 45 (49, 53) A. Row 4: P 45 (49, 53) A, p 9 B. Continue in this manner, working 1 st more in B and 1 st less in A every other row 10 times more. Work 4 rows even as established, then work 1 st less in B and 1 st more in A every other row

until 9 (10, 11) B sts remain. Work these 9 (10, 11) sts in B for remainder of Front. **AT THE SAME TIME,** start Right Side Patch ½" below start of armhole shaping. **RIGHT SIDE PATCH: Row 1:** Work to within 14 sts from seam edge, attach another B ball, k 3 B, complete remainder of row with A. **Row 2:** P in colors as established. **Row 3:** Work to within 15 sts from end, k 5 B, complete row with A. Continue in this manner to work 1 B st more on each side every other row until there are 11 B sts. **AT SAME TIME,** bind off and dec for armhole as for Back. When there are 11 B sts in patch, work even 4 rows as established, then **at beg of patch pattern only,** work 1 st less in B and 1 st more in A every other row 4 times. Work remainder of right side with A—40 (44, 48) sts. When armhole measures 3 (3½, 4)", **SHAPE NECK:** Work 13 (14, 15) sts, place remaining sts on a holder. At neck edge, dec 1 st every other row 4 times—9 (10, 11) sts. Work to shoulder as for Back. **SHAPE SHOULDER:** At arm edge, bind off 5 sts once, 4 (5, 6) sts once. Leave center 14 (16, 18) sts on a holder, place remaining 13 (14, 15) sts on needle. Attach yarn at neck edge, work to correspond to other side, reversing shaping.

SLEEVES: Left Sleeve: With No. 6 needles and A, cast on 34 (34, 38) sts. Work in k 2, p 2 ribbing for 1¼". Change to No. 8 needle and stock. st. Inc 1 st each end every 1" 4 (5, 5) times. **AT THE SAME TIME,** when 4¼" from beg, start patch. **Row 1:** With A, k to within 8 sts from end, k 8 B. **Row 2:** P 8 B, p remainder of row with A. **Row 3:** With A, k to within 9 sts from end, k 9 B. Continue in this manner to work 1 st more in B and 1 st less in A every other row 13 times more. Work 4 rows even in colors as established, then work 1 st less in B and 1 st more in A every other row 4 times. Remainder of sleeve worked with A—42 (44, 48) sts. When sleeve measures 8½ (10, 11½)" from beg, or desired length, **SHAPE CAP:** Bind off 4 sts beg next 2 rows. Dec 1 st each end every other row until cap is 2¾ (3, 3½)". Bind off 2 sts beg next 4 rows. Bind off. **Right Sleeve:** Work to correspond to Left Sleeve, reversing side of patch.

NECKBAND: Sew left shoulder seam. With No. 6 needle, C and right side facing, pick up and k 54 (58, 62) sts around neck (this includes sts on holders). Work in k 2, p 2 ribbing for 1". Bind off in ribbing.

FINISHING: Sew shoulder and neckband in corresponding colors. Sew side and sleeve seams in corresponding colors. Sew in sleeves. Steam very lightly. **DO NOT PRESS OR BLOCK.** Cut a piece of felt 1½" x 1". With a laundry marking pencil, write "SPOT", or desired name on felt. Sew felt piece to neckband as shown. **Note:** Remove felt piece when sweater is washed.

HAT

With No. 6 needles and B, cast on 88 (88, 92) sts. Work in k 1, p 1 ribbing for 1¼". Change to No. 8 needle and stock. st. Work even until 3 (3, 3½)" from beg, ending with a p row. **PATCH: Row 1:** K 32 (32, 34) B, attach A, k 24 A, attach another B, k 32 (32, 34) B. **Row 2:** P 32 (32, 34) B, p 24 A, p 32 (32, 34) B. **Row 3:** K 31 (31, 33) B, k 26 A, k 31 (31, 33) B. **Row 4:** P 31 (31, 33) B, p 26 A, p 31 (31, 33) B. Continue in this manner, working 1 st more of A on each side of patch until there are 30 A sts in patch. Work even 10 rows in colors as established. Work 1 st less of A on each side of patch and 1 st more of B on each side 6 times, then work remainder of cap with B. **AT THE SAME TIME,** when 4½ (5, 5)" from beg, **SHAPE TOP: Row 1:** Dec 8 sts evenly spaced across row (if dec comes within A spot, then work it). **Row 2:** Work even. Repeat the last 2 rows until 8 (8, 8) sts remain. For size 2 and 4 only, p 2 tog across last row—4 sts. For size 6, p across last row. Break yarn, leaving a long strand.

FINISHING: With a tapestry needle, draw yarn through remaining sts, draw tog and sew back seam. **EARS:** Make 2. With No. 8 needle and B, cast on 4 sts. Work stock. st, increasing 1 st each end every other row until 24 sts on needle. Work even 2". Bind off. With tapestry needle and B, sew a running st along bound off edge and draw tightly tog. Sew on ears as shown. **DO NOT BLOCK OR PRESS.**

SIZES: Directions are for small size (4-6). Changes for medium size (8-10) are in parentheses.

MATERIALS: Bernat Krysta, 90% Orlon®, 10% Acrylic Nylon, (2-oz balls): 6 (7) balls #6659 Natural (A); 2 balls each #6620 Walnut (B) and #6618 Chestnut (C); 1 ball #6655 Copper (D). Knitting Needles, 1 pair each Nos. 11 and 15 OR SIZES TO OBTAIN GAUGE. Crochet Hook, Size K.

GAUGE: No. 15 needles — 2 sts = 1″; 5 rows = 1″. No. 11 needles — 5 sts = 2″; 7 rows = 2″.

MEASUREMENTS: Width around chest, not including front borders — 25 (28)″; sleeves at upperarms — 9½ (12½)″.

Note 1: Work with 2 strands of same color unless otherwise specified.

Note 2: On K rows following charts, start at A and work to B; rep between A and B across, ending at number of sts for size being made. On P rows start at number of sts for size and work to A; rep between B and A across, ending at A. Body sts are at lower edge of charts; sleeve sts are at top of charts. Carry unused colors loosely across back of work.

BODY: With No. 15 needles and B, cast on 51 (57) sts. P 1 row. In st st (k 1 row, p 1 row) work 4 rows of Chart 1. With A, work 4 rows. Work 15 rows of Chart 2, ending with a k row. **Next Row:** With A, p 9 (11), bind off next 5 sts, p until 23 (25) sts from bind off, bind off 5 sts, finish row. Place sts on a holder, do not cut yarn.

SLEEVES: With No. 15 needles and B, cast on 19 (25) sts. Work same as body through row 15 of Chart 2. **Next Row:** With A, bind off 2 sts, p to last 2 sts, bind off 2 sts. Cut yarn. Place sts on a holder.

Raglan Shaping: Place sts of left front, sleeve, back, sleeve and right front on No. 15 needle. **Joining Row:** With A, k

9 (11) sts of right front, place a marker on needle, k 1, place a marker on needle, k 13 (19), place a marker, k 1, place a marker, k 23 (25), place a marker, k 1, place a marker, k 13 (19), place a marker, k 1, place a marker, k 9 (11) — 71 (89) sts. **Row 2:** Slipping markers every row, p across. **Row 3:** *K to within 2 sts of next marker, k 2 tog, k 1, sl 1, k 1, psso, rep from * 3 times, k to end. Rep Rows 2 and 3 until 23 (25) sts rem, end with a p row. K next row and dec 2 (4) sts evenly spaced—21 sts. Bind off.

LOWER BORDER: With crochet hook join 2 strands of A in first st at lower left front, ch 1, * sk 1 st, sc in next st,

sc in skipped st; rep from * across. Ch 1, turn. Rep last row 4 times more. Fasten off. Work 1 row of same edging along sleeve edges.

LEFT FRONT BORDER: With No. 11 needles and a single strand of A, cast on 17 sts. **Row 1:** P. **Row 2:** K 8, sl 1 as to p, k 8. Rep these 2 rows until band, when stretched slightly, is same length as front edge, end with a p row. Cut yarn. Sew inner edge of band along left front.

RIGHT FRONT BAND: Work same as left front band. Do not cut yarn. Sew inner edge to right front.

COLLAR: K 8, sl 1, k 8 across right front band, pick up and k 34 sts around neck edge, k 8, sl 1, k 8 across left front band — 68 sts. P 1 row. **Rows 1-4:** K 1 row, p 1 row, twice. **Row 5:** (K 2 A, 2 D) twice, sl 1, * 2A, 2D; rep from * to last 11 sts, 2 A, sl 1, (2 D, 2 A) twice. **Row 6:** P back in colors as set up. **Rows 7-8:** K 1 row, p 1 row. **Row 9:** K 4A, 2D, 2A, sl 1, * 2D, 2 A; rep from * to last 9 sts, sl 1, 2 A, 2 D, 4 A. **Row 10:** P back in colors. **Rows 11-14:** K 1 row, p 1 row, twice. **Row 15:** Bind off 17 sts, p to last 17 sts, k 17. **Row 16:** Bind off 17 sts, p across — 34 sts. **Rows 17-20:** K 1 row, p 1 row, twice. **Rows 21-22:** Work from * of Row 9 and 10. **Rows 23-24:** K 1 row, p 1 row. **Rows 25-26:** Rep from * of Row 5 and 6. Work 5 rows st st. Bind off on a p row.

BELT: With No. 11 needles and single strand of A, cast on 7 sts. **Row 1:** Sl 1, k 2, sl 1, k 3. **Row 2:** Sl 1, p 6. Rep these 2 rows until belt measures desired length. Bind off.

FINISHING: With right sides tog, fold front border sts in half. Sew bound-off sts and cast on sts tog. Turn to right side. Sew collar to neck edge. Sew bands to front edges. Weave sts of bands along the sides of the collar. Fold belt in half lengthwise and sew edges tog.

KEY:
— A, NATURAL
— B, WALNUT
— C, CHESTNUT

SLEEVE 25 STS 19 STS CHART 1 ROW 1

BODY 57 STS 51 STS B A

19 (25) STS SLEEVE CHART 2

BODY 51 (57) STS ROW 1 REPEAT B A

SIZES: Leggings and Sweater directions are for size 1. Changes for sizes 2, 4 and 6 are in parentheses. Cap directions are for small (1-2) size. Changes for medium (3-4) size are in parentheses.

MATERIALS: Brunswick Germantown Knitting Worsted (4 oz skn): 4 (4-5-5) skns #441 Turquoise Heather or #485 Peach Glow Heather and Brunswick Promfret Sport (2 oz pull skn): 5 (5-6-6) skns #5000 Cream or #585 Peach Glow Heather. Knitting Needles, 1 pair each of Nos. 7 and 9 OR SIZE TO OBTAIN GAUGE.

NOTE: Work with one strand each of Knitting Worsted and Sport Yarn held tog throughout; using Turquoise with Cream or #485 Peach Glow Heather with #585 Peach Glow Heather.

GAUGE: On No. 9 needles — 17 sts = 4"; 5 rows = 1".

BLOCKING MEASUREMENTS: Chest — 24 (25-26-28)". Width of back or front at underarm — 12 (12½-13-14)". Width of sleeve at upper arm — 10 (10½-11-11½)". Width of leggings at hips 24 (25-28-31)"

SWEATER

BACK: With one strand each of Knitting Worsted and Sport Yarn held tog as directed, using No. 7 needles, cast on 50 (53-56-59) sts. **Row 1 (wrong side):** K 2, * p 1, k 2; rep from * across. **Row 2:** P 2, * with yarn in back sl 1, p 2; rep from * across. **Rows 3-11:** Rep these 2 rows alternately 4 more times, then rep Row 1 once more for ribbing. Change to No. 9 needles and k across, increasing 0 (1-0-1) st — 50 (54-56-60) sts. Starting with a p row, work in stockinette st (p 1 row, k 1 row) until length is 7½ (8¼-9½-10½)" from beg, ending with a p row.

RAGLAN ARMHOLES: Rows 1-2: Continuing in stockinette st, bind off 3 sts at beg of each row. **Row 3:** K 2, k 2 tog, k across to within last 4 sts, sl 1, k 1, psso, k 2. **Row 4:** P across. Rep last 2 rows alternately 14 (15-16-17) more times — 14 (16-16-18) sts rem. Place rem sts on a st holder.

FRONT: Work same as for Back until the 11 rows of ribbing have been completed. **Next row:** K, increasing 4 (5-4-5) sts evenly spaced across row — 54 (58-60-64) sts. Change to No. 9 needles and work pat as follows: **Row 1 (wrong side):** P 10 (10-10-12), place a marker on a needle; **k 2, p 8, k 2 — cable panel;** place a marker on a needle; p 10 (14-16-16), place a marker on a needle; k 2, p 8, k 2, for cable panel; place a marker on a needle; p 10 (10-10-12). **Row 2:** * K to next marker, slip marker; p 2, **sl next 2 sts onto a dp needle and hold in back of work, k next 2 sts, k the 2 sts on dp needle, sl next 2 sts onto dp needle and hold in front of work, k next 2 sts, k the 2 sts on dp needle—cable made;** p 2, slip marker; rep from * once; k rem sts. **Rows 3, 5 and 7:** * P to next marker, slip marker; k 2, p 8, k 2, slip marker; rep from * once; p rem sts. **Always slip markers. Row 4:** * K to next marker, p 2, k 8, p 2; rep from * once; k rem sts. **Row 6:** Rep Row 4. **Row 8:** * K to next marker, p 2, sl next 2 sts onto dp needle and hold in front of work, k next 2 sts, k the 2 sts on dp needle, sl next 2 sts onto dp needle and hold in back of work, k next 2 sts, k the 2 sts on dp needle, p 2; rep from * once; k rem sts. Slipping markers already

placed, rep last 8 rows (Rows 1 through 8) for pat. Work in pat until length is 7½ (8½-9½-10½)"; ending with a wrong-side row.

RAGLAN ARMHOLES: Rows 1-2: Keeping continuity of cable panels throughout, bind off 3 sts at beg of each row. **Row 3:** K 2, k 2 tog; work in pat across to within last 4 sts, sl 1, k 1, psso, k 2. **Row 4:** Work in pat. Rep last 2 rows until 28 (30-30-32) sts rem, ending with a wrong-side row.

NECK: Next Row: Decreasing one st at beg of row as before, work until there are 10 sts on right-hand needle; attach another double strand and work over next 6 (8-8-10) sts, place these last sts made on a st holder; complete row, decreasing at end of row as before. Working both sides at the same time with separate skns, continue to dec one st at each armhole edge as before on every right-side row 4 more times, **at the same time,** dec one st at each neck edge every other row 3 (3-3-4) times. Bind off.

SLEEVES: With one strand each of Knitting Worsted and Sport Yarn held tog, using No. 7 needles, cast on 29 (32-32-35) sts. Work same as for Back until 11 rows of ribbing have been completed. **Next row:** K across, increasing 3 (2-2-1) sts evenly spaced across—32 (34-34-36) sts. Change to No. 9 needles and work in pat as follows: **Row 1:** P 11 (11-11-12), place a marker on a needle; k 2, p 8, k 2, place a marker on a needle; p rem sts. Working cable panel over sts between markers same as for Front throughout sleeve and working all other sts in stockinette st, inc one st at each end every 4th (6th-6th-6th) row until there are 42 (44-46-48) sts on needle. Work even until total length is 8¼ (9-10¼-11½)" from beg, ending with a wrong-side row.

RAGLAN TOP SHAPING: Work same as Raglan Armholes of Front until Row 3 has been completed. **Next 3 rows:** Work 3 rows even in pattern. Now rep Rows 3-4 of Front Raglan Armholes with 8 (8-10-10) sts rem. Place rem sts on a st holder.

FINISHING: Block pieces to measurements. Sew side and sleeve seams. Sew in left sleeve; sew right sleeve to front only. **Neckband:** With right side facing, using double strand as directed and No. 7 needles, pick up and k 56 (59-65-71) sts along entire neck edge, including sts on holders. **Row 1 (wrong side):** K 2, * p 1, k 2; rep from * across. **Row 2:** P 2, * with yarn in back sl 1, p 2; rep from * across. Rep last 2 rows alternately for 3½ (4-4½-5)". Bind off loosely in pat. Sew back right sleeve seam, including neckband.

LEGGINGS

RIGHT SECTION: Start at lower edge with one strand each of Knitting Worsted and Sport Yarn held tog, using No. 7 needles, cast on 32 (35-38-44) sts. Work same as for Back of Sweater until the 11 rows of ribbing have been completed, increasing 0 (1-2-0) sts on last row. Change to No. 7 needles and work as follows: **Row 1:** K 9 (10-11-12), with yarn in back sl 1, k 14 (16-18-20), with yarn in back sl 1, k 7 (8-9-10)—2 ridges started. **Row 2:** P across. **Rows 3-6:** Rep last 2 rows twice. **Row 7 (Inc Row):** K 2, inc in next st, k across to within next ridge, with yarn in back sl 1, k 5 (6-7-8), inc in next st, place a marker on needle; k 2, place a marker on needle; inc in next st, k to next ridge, sl 1 as

before, k to within last 2 sts, inc in next st, k 1—4 incs made. **Always slip markers. 8th Row:** P across. Keeping continuity of the two sl-st ridges on every right-side row and working all other sts in stockinette st (k 1 row, p 1 row) work 4 (4-6-6) rows even. **Next row (Inc Row):** K 2, inc in next st, k to next ridge, sl 1, k to within one st before next marker, inc in next st, k 2, inc in next st, k to next ridge, sl 1, k to last 2 sts, inc in next st, k 1—40 (44-48-52) sts. Rep this Inc Row every 8th (8th-10th-10th) row until there are 56 (60-68-76) sts. Continuing ridges throughout, work even until length is 10 (11¾-14¼-16½)", ending with a wrong-side row.

Crotch Shaping: Row 1: Bind off 2 sts—mark this end for front edge; complete row. **Row 2:** Bind off 3 sts—mark this end for back edge; complete row. **Row 3:** Bind off 1 (1-2-4) sts; complete row. **Row 4:** P across. Now dec one st at front edge every 10th row 3 times; **at the same time,** dec one st at back edge every 4th row 3 (4-5-5) times—44 (47-53-59) sts. Work even until total length is 17½ (19¾-22-25)", ending with a right-side row.

BACK SHAPING: Row 1: Work across to within last 22 sts. Turn. **Row 2:** Work to end of row. **Row 3:** Work to within last 4 sts of last row. Turn. **Row 4:** Work to end of row. Rep last 2 rows 3 more times. Change to No. 7 needles and working over all sts, work 9 rows of ribbing same as for Back of Sweater. Bind off loosely.

LEFT SECTION: Work to correspond with Right Section, reversing shaping.

FINISHING: Block pieces to measurements. Sew center back and center front seams from crotch markers to top edge. Sew leg seams.

CAP

Start at lower edge with double strand as directed and No. 7 needles, cast on 77 (86) sts. Work same as for Back of Sweater until the 11 rows of ribbing have been completed, increasing 5 (4) sts evenly spaced on last row—82 (90) sts. Change to No. 9 needles and work as follows: **Row 1:** P 8 (9), place a marker on needle, **k 2, p 8, k 2—cable panel;** * place a marker on a needle; p 15 (18), place a marker on needle; **k 2, p 8, k 2—cable panel;** rep from * once; place a marker on needle; p 8 (9)—3 cable panels started. Working cable panels same as on Front of Sweater (starting with 2nd row of pat) and working all other sts in stockinette st, work even until length is 5¼ (6½)" from beg, ending with a wrong-side row. **Top Shaping: Row 1:** K 4 (5), * sl 1, k 1, psso, k 2 tog, p 2 tog, work in pat over next 8 sts, p 2 tog, sl 1, k 1, psso, k 2 tog, k to within 4 sts before next marker; rep from * across, ending last rep with k 4 (5)—64 (72) sts. **Rows 2-3-4:** Work even in pat, having 10 sts on each panel. **Row 5:** K 2 (3), * (k 2 tog) twice; p 1, k 2, (k 2 tog) twice, p 1, (k 2 tog) twice; k to within 4 sts before next marker; rep from * across, ending with k 2 (3) —46 (54) sts. Work 1 row even. Working in stockinette st over all sts, dec 11 (13) sts evenly spaced on next row and every other row thereafter until 13 (15) sts rem. Break off, leaving a 12-inch length of yarn. Thread this end into a large-eyed needle and slip through rem sts. Pull tightly and fasten, sew back seam. Make pompom, sew to cap.

SPIRAL PATTERN KNITS

SPIRAL PAT 1: (Worked over a multiple of 8 sts) **Rnds 1, 2, 3 and 4:** * K4, P4, rep from * around. **Rnds 5, 6, 7 and 8:** P1, * K4, P4, rep from * around, end K4, P3. **Rnds 9, 10, 11 and 12:** P2, * K4, P4, rep from * around, end K4, P2. **Rnds 13, 14, 15 and 16:** P3, * K4, P4, rep from * around, end K4, P1. **Rnds** 17, 18, 19 and 20: * P4, K4, rep from * around. **Rnds 21, 22, 23 and 24:** K1, * P4, K4, rep from * around, end P4, K3. **Rnds 25, 26, 27 and 28:** K2, * P4, K4, rep from * around, end P4, K2. **Rnds 29, 30, 31 and 32:** K3, * P4, K4, rep from * around, end P4, K1. Rep these 32 rnds for Spiral Pat 1.

SPIRAL PAT 2: (Worked over a multiple of 6 sts) **Rnds 1, 2, 3 and 4:** * K3, P3, rep from * around. **Rnds 5, 6, 7 and 8:** P1, * K3, P3, rep from * around, end K3, P2. **Rnds 9, 10, 11 and 12:** P2, * K3, P3, rep from * around, end K3, P1. **Rnds 13, 14, 15 and 16:** * P3, K3, rep from * around. **Rnds 17, 18, 19 and 20:** K1, * P3, K3, rep from * around, end P3, K2. **Rnds 21, 22, 23 and 24:** K2, * P3, K3, rep from * around, end P3, K1. Rep these 24 rnds for Spiral Pat 2.

CHILD AND ADULT HAT, MITTENS AND SOCKS SPIRAL KNIT SET

SIZES: Directions are for child's. Changes for adult's are in parentheses. **Hat:** One size fits all.

MATERIALS: 4 Ply yarns. Sets are worked using 8 different colors. However, knitters are free to create their own stripe pat using any number of yarns desired. 16 oz. of yarn or 2 oz. of colors A, B, C, D, E, F, G and H. For pictured Child Set, variations of Greens, Browns and Golds are used. For Adult Set, variations of Reds, Purples and Pinks are used. No. 7 and No. 8 dp needles, OR SIZE TO OBTAIN GAUGE. 1 tapestry needle.

GAUGE: 5 sts = 1", 7 rnds = 1".

NOTE: Stripe pat shown on Adult models is given for each piece.

HAT

STRIPE PAT: 14 rnds A, 2 rnds H, 3 rnds A, 18 rnds D, 1 rnd G, 2 rnds H, 10 rnds C, 6 rnds G, 4 rnds F, 3 rnds H, 1 rnd E, complete with H.

With No. 7 dp needles and A cast on 96 sts. Divide sts evenly on 3 dp needles. Place marker between first and last needle for beg of rnds. Join being careful not to twist sts. **Rnd 1:** * K2, P2, rep from * around. Work to 2½" or desired rib length. Change to No. 8 dp needles and **Spiral Pat 1.** Work to 6" from beg or desired length before top shaping.

SHAPE TOP: Dec Rnd 1: * K2 tog, K2, P2 tog, P2, rep from * around. 72 sts. Keeping to Spiral pat, work K3, P3 for 2". **Dec Rnd 2:** * K2 tog, K1, P2 tog, P1, rep from * around. 48 sts. Keeping to Spiral pat, work K2, P2 for 1". **Dec Rnd 3:** * K2 tog, P2 tog, rep from * around. 24 sts. Work in K1, P1 rib for 2 rnds.

Break off yarn leaving a long strand for sewing. Thread yarn to tapestry needle and draw through sts on needle. Pull tight and sew down on wrong side.

MITTENS

STRIPE PAT: 12 rnds A, 3 rnds H, 9 rnds A, 4 rnds D, 12 rnds A, 12 rnds D, 4 rnds G, 2 rnds H, 9 rnds C, * 3 rnds H, 7 rnds G, 4 rnds F, for longer mittens rep from * to desired length. Work thumb stripes to correspond to hand stripes.

CUFF: With No. 7 dp needles and A cast on 40 sts. Work same as hat until rib band measures 5½".

WRISTBAND: Dec Rnd: * K2 tog, P2 tog, rep from * around. 20 sts. Work in K1, P1 rib for 3 rnds. K1 rnd, inc 1 st in each st. 40 sts. Change to No. 8 dp needles and **Spiral pat 1.** Work 4 rnds, or desired length to beg of thumb gusset.

GUSSET: Rnd 1: Place marker, K 3 sts, place marker, keeping to pat complete rnd.

NOTE: Sts between markers are worked in Stock st (K every rnd) and remaining sts are worked in Spiral pat. Work 1 rnd. **Rnd 3:** Sl marker, inc 1 st in next st, K1, inc 1 st in next st, sl marker, work in pat around. 5 sts between markers. Continue to inc 1 st after first marker and before last marker every other row 2 times more. 9 sts between markers. Sl these 9 sts on a holder to be worked later for thumb.

HAND: Cast on 3 sts at beg of first needle, work in pat around. Working cast on sts into pat, work to 4(5)" above gusset or 1" less than desired length to top of mitten.

SHAPE TOP: Dec Rnd 1: Rep Dec Rnd 1 of hat. 30 sts. Keeping to Spiral pat work 3 rnds. **Dec Rnd 2:** Rep Dec Rnd 2 of hat. 20 sts. Work 3 rnds. Break off yarn. Complete as top of hat.

THUMB: Sl 9 sts from holder and divide evenly on 2 No. 8 dp needles, on a 3rd dp needle cast on 5 sts. 14 sts. Working rnd, work in Stock st to desired length.

SHAPE TOP: * K2 tog, rep from * around. Break off yarn. Complete as top of hat. Sew seam at base of thumb.

SOCKS

STRIPE PAT: 14 rnds A, * 6 rnds B, 12 rnds C, 6 rnds B, 4 rnds D, 16 rnds E, 4 rnds D, 8 rnds F, 4 rnds G, 12 rnds D, 3 rnds H, for longer socks rep from * to desired length. With No. 7 dp needles and A cast on 40 sts. Work same as hat until rib band measures 1¾" for short socks and 3" for long socks. Change to No. 8 dp needles and **Spiral Pat 1.** Work to 12(14)" for short socks and 14(16½)" for long socks, or 3 inches less than desired length to tip of toe. Change to Stock st. Work 1"

SHAPE TIP: Dec Rnd 1: K to last 3 sts on first needle, K2 tog, K1, K to last 3 sts on 2nd needle, K2 tog, K1, K to last 3 sts on 3rd needle, K2 tog, K1. Rep this dec rnd every other rnd 7 times more. 16 sts. **Dec rnd 2:** * K3, K2 tog, rep from * around, end K1. 13 sts. Work 1 rnd. **Dec Rnd 3:** * K2, K2 tog, rep from * around. 10 sts. Break off yarn. Complete as top of hat.

continued on page 126

TODDLER SWEATER, HAT, MITTENS AND SOCKS SPIRAL KNIT SET

SIZES: Directions are for Size 1. Changes for sizes 2 and 3 are in parentheses.

MATERIALS: Sweater: Any 100% Wool, 4 ply Knitting Worsted, 4(5,5) ozs. Natural (A), 1 oz. Dark Brown (C). Bernat Mohair Plus, 1 ball #5316 Mink (B). **Hat, Mittens and Socks:** 6 ozs. A, 2 ozs. B, 1 oz. each of C and Bernat Mohair Plus #5326 Pastel Pink (D). Nos. 5, 6, 7 and 8 dp needles. Nos. 4, 7 and 8 straight needles OR SIZES TO OBTAIN GIVEN GAUGES. 1 small button. 1 tapestry needle. Crochet hook size 0.

GAUGE: On No. 8 needles 5 sts = 1 inch, 6 rows = 1 inch. On No. 6 needles 5½ sts = 1 inch, 7 rows = 1 inch.

SWEATER

BACK: With No. 7 straight needles and A cast on 52(58–62) sts. Work in K2, P2 rib. Work 5 rows A, 3 rows B, 1 row C, 2 rows B, 8 rows A. Change to No. 8 straight needles and Stock st. Dec 1 st at beg of first row, 51(57–61) sts. Work 7 rows A, 1 row C, 2 rows B, 1 row A, 2 rows B, 1 row C, 6 rows A, 3 rows B, 2 rows C, 1 row B. Break off B and C. Work in A only to 7½(8–8½)″ from beg, ending with a wrong side row.

SHAPE ARMHOLES: Bind off 2(3–3) sts at beg of next 2 rows. **Dec Row 1:** K1, sl1, K1, psso, K to last 3 sts, K2 tog, K1. Work 1 row. Rep these 2 rows 7(7–8) times more. 31(35–37) sts. **Dec Row 2:** K1, sl1, K2 tog, psso, K to last 3 sts, K3 tog, K1. Work 1 row. Rep these last 2 rows 0(1–1) times more. 27(27–29) sts. Sl these sts on a holder to be worked later for neck.

FRONT: Work same as back.

TURTLENECK: With No. 8 dp needles K 27(27–29) sts off back holder, cast on 3(3–4) sts for top of sleeve edge, K 27(27–29) sts off front holder, cast on 3(3–4) sts for top of other sleeve edge. Divide these sts evenly on 3 dp needles, place marker between first and last needle for start of rnds. Working around, work in **Spiral Pat 2.** Work 19 rnds A, 3 rnds B, 1 rnd C, 3 rnds B, 3 rnds A. Bind off in pat with A. Sew side seams.

SLEEVES: From right side with No. 8 dp needles, beg at side seam pick up 48(54–54) sts evenly around entire armhole edge.

Place a marker. Divide these sts evenly on 3 dp needles. Working around work in **Spiral Pat 2.** Work 11 rnds A, 1 rnd B, 2 rnds C, 3 rnds B, 8 rnds A, 1 rnd C, 3 rnds B, 1 rnd A, 2 rnds B, 1 rnd C, work in A until sleeve measures 6(7–8)″ from beg or 2″ less than desired length. **AT SAME TIME** When sleeve measures 1″ and being sure to keep to pat, dec 1 st each side of marker, then every ¾″ 5(6–6) times more, 36(40–40) sts. Remove marker. Change to No. 7 dp needles and K2, P2 rib. Work 4 rnds A, 2 rnds B, 1 rnd C, 3 rnds B. Work with A only until rib band measures 2″. Bind off in rib.

FINISHING: Block sweater lightly.

HAT

With No. 7 dp needles and A cast on 72 sts. Divide these sts evenly on 3 dp needles. Place marker between first and last needle for start of rnds. Join, being careful not to twist sts. Working rnd, work in K2, P2 rib. Work 6 rnds A, 1 rnd C, 2 rnds D, 1 rnd C, 4 rnds A. Change to No. 8 dp needles and **Spiral Pat 2.** Work 8 rnds A, 3 rnds B, 1 rnd C, 2 rnds B, 2 rnds A, 2 rnds D, 3 rnds A, 2 rnds B, 1 rnd C, 3 rnds B. Break off B, C and D. Work in pat with A only. Work to 7″ from beg.

SHAPE TOP: Dec Rnd 1: Keeping to pat * K1, K2 tog, P1, P2 tog, rep from * around. Keeping to pat work K2, P2 for 1″. **Dec Rnd 2:** * K2 tog, P2 tog, rep from * around. 36 sts. Work 1 rnd. Break off yarn leaving a strand for sewing. Thread yarn through a tapestry needle and draw through sts on needles. Pull tight, and sew down at back of work.

BUTTON STRAP: With No. 4 straight needle cast on 26 sts. Work in K2, P2 rib for 3 rows. Cast on 2 sts at end of next row. Working new sts into rib pat work 2 rows. Bind off 2 sts at beg of next row. Work 2 rows. Bind off in rib.

BUTTONHOLE STRAP: Work same as Button strap to 1 row after the 2–st cast on row.

BUTTONHOLE: Work in rib to 6 sts before point edge, yo, work 2 sts tog, work to end.
Next Row: Bind off 2 sts at beg of row, work

in rib to end, working yo into pat. Complete as for Button Strap. Sew straps to hat at inside of rib band. Sew on button. Block lightly.

MITTENS

With No. 5 dp needles and A cast on 36 sts. Work same as hat rib band, in A only to 1¾″ from beg. **EYELET RND:** * K2, yo, P2 tog, rep from * around. Working yos into rib pat, with A work 2 rnds. Change to No. 6 dp needles and **Spiral Pat 2.** Work 3 rnds B, 1 rnd C, 2 rnds A, 3 rnds D, 3 rnds A, 1 rnd C, 4 rnds B. Break off B, C and D. Work with A only. Work to 5″ from beg or 1″ less than desired length to tip. Change to Stock st (K every rnd). K 1 rnd.

SHAPE TOP: Dec Rnd 1: * K4, K2 tog, rep from * around. Work 1 rnd. **Dec Rnd 2:** * K3, K2 tog, rep from * around. Work 1 rnd. **Dec Rnd 3:** * K2, K2 tog, rep from * around. Work 1 rnd. **Dec Rnd 4:** * K1, K2 tog, rep from * around. Break off yarn leaving a strand for sewing. Complete as top of hat.

TIES (make 2): With 0 hook and 1 strand of A and B held tog, make a chain about 20″ long. Fasten off.

FRINGE (make 4): Cut strands of A, B, C and D about 3″ long. Fold in half. About ¼″ below loop edge wind a strand of A around tightly. Knot A tog. Trim fringe. Weave ties thru eyelet rnd. Sew 1 fringe to each tie end.

SOCKS

With No. 7 dp needles and A cast on 36 sts. Work same as hat rib band, working 7 rnds A, 1 rnd C, 2 rnds D, 1 rnd C, 3 rnds A. Change to No. 8 dp needles and **Spiral Pat 2.** Work 13 rnds A, 4 rnds B, 1 rnd C, 3 rnds B, 6 rnds A, 2 rnds D. Break off B, C and D. Work with A only. Work to 8½″ from beg or 2″ less than desired length to tip of toe. Change to Stock st. K 1 rnd.

SHAPE TIP: Dec Rnd 1: K to last 3 sts on first needle, K2 tog, K1, K to last 3 sts on 2nd needle, K2 tog, K1, K to last 3 sts on 3rd needle, K 2 tog, K1. K 1 rnd. Rep these 2 rnds 3 times more. Beg with Dec Rnd 1 of mittens, complete socks as mittens.

BASHFUL LION

MATERIALS: Fleisher's Twin-Pak Knitting Worsted (4 oz paks): 1 pak each of colors A—#55 Orange, B—#91 Apricot Brandy, C—#358 Antique Gold; a few yards each of leftover yarn or embroidery floss for face: magenta, black, white, emerald, Apricot Brandy. Foam or cotton batting for stuffing. Knitting Needles, No. 11 OR SIZE TO OBTAIN GAUGE. Tapestry needle.

GAUGE: 3 sts = 1"; 7 rows = 2".

NOTE: Use 2 strands of yarn throughout. † (dagger)—used in same way as * when another symbol is needed.

BACK: With No. 11 needles and double strand of A, cast on 7 sts for top of head. **Row 1** (wrong side): P. **Row 2:** Inc 1 st in first st, k to within 2 sts of end, inc 1 st in next st, k 1—9 sts. Repeat last 2 rows 3 times—15 sts. Work 2 rows even. **Next Row:** P to within last 2 sts, p 2 tog. Place marker on needle. **Next Row:** Cast on 21 sts for body, k to

end—35 sts. Work even in stockinette st (p 1 row, K 1 row) until 18 rows from marker, end with p row.

DIVIDE FOR LEGS: Next Row: K 4 sts, bind off next 4 sts, k until 4 sts from bind off, bind off the next 11 sts, k until 4 sts from last bind off, bind off next 4 sts, k to end.

FIRST LEG: Next Row: † P 3, inc 1 st in last st—5 sts. Work stockinette st 7 rows more, end on right side. **Next Row:** Work a popcorn in first st as follows; k 1 in the front, the back, the front and the back of st, pass the first 3 of these sts over last st; * k 1, popcorn in next st. Repeat from * once. **Next Row:** Bind off.

2ND LEG: Next Row: Wrong side facing, join yarn at beg of next 4 sts on left needle. Inc 1 st in first st, p 3—5 sts. Complete as for first leg †.

HIND LEGS: Wrong side facing, join yarn at beg of next 4 sts on left needle. Repeat between †'s once.

FRONT: Work same as for back, shaping to correspond.

FINISHING: Embroider face following color illustration and Diagram. Weave front and back pieces together leaving opening on back for stuffing. Run strand of yarn through bound-off sts on each leg, draw up tightly and fasten off. Stuff and weave opening tog.

TAIL: Cut 12, 24" strands of A, pull 12 strands half way through back end sts on body, separate into 3 groups of 4 strands each and make a braid 3½" long. Fasten securely leaving remaining ends loose. Cut 4, 5" strands each of colors B and C, tie strand in center and attach to end of braid.

MANE: Using B and C, wind yarn around a 4½" cardboard, cut at one end. Knot 4 strand fringe around face and head and on back of head, alternating fringes of B and C as illustrated. Use three strands each (3" long) of color B for whiskers; attach to either side of face.

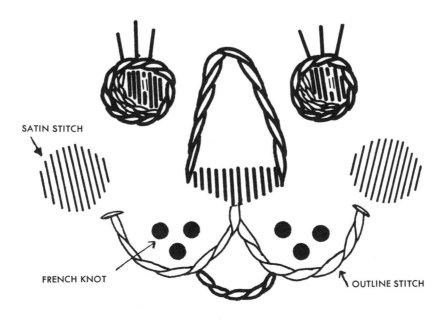

SATIN STITCH

FRENCH KNOT

OUTLINE STITCH